COMPUTER Applications

for Microsoft® Office 365
2019 Edition

Review and Assessment

Denise Seguin
Fanshawe College, London, Ontario

PARADIGM
EDUCATION SOLUTIONS

St. Paul

Vice President, Content and Digital Solutions: Christine Hurney
Director of Content Development, Computer Technology: Cheryl Drivdahl
Developmental Editor: Jennifer Gehlhar
Director of Production: Timothy W. Larson
Production Editor: Carrie Rogers
Design and Production Specialist: Jack Ross
Interior Design: Jack Ross
Cover Design: Jack Ross
Page Layout: Jack Ross
Photo Researcher and Illustrator: Melora Pappas
Copy Editor: Penny Stuart
Proofreader: Eric Braem
Tester: Julia Basham and Janet Blum
Indexer: Terry Casey
Vice President, Director of Digital Products: Chuck Bratton
Digital Projects Manager: Tom Modl
Digital Solutions Manager: Gerry Yumul
Senior Director of Digital Products and Onboarding: Christopher Johnson
Supervisor of Digital Products and Onboarding: Ryan Isdahl
Vice President, Marketing: Lara Weber McLellan
Marketing and Communications Manager: Selena Hicks

Care has been taken to verify the accuracy of information presented in this book. However, the authors, editors, and publisher cannot accept responsibility for web, email, newsgroup, or chat room subject matter or content, or for consequences from the application of the information in this book, and make no warranty, expressed or implied, with respect to its content.

Trademarks: Microsoft is a trademark or registered trademark of Microsoft Corporation in the United States and/or other countries. Some of the product names and company names included in this book have been used for identification purposes only and may be trademarks or registered trade names of their respective manufacturers and sellers. The authors, editors, and publisher disclaim any affiliation, association, or connection with, or sponsorship or endorsement by, such owners.

Cover Photo Credit: © Shutterstock/vlastas

We have made every effort to trace the ownership of all copyrighted material and to secure permission from copyright holders. In the event of any question arising as to the use of any material, we will be pleased to make the necessary corrections in future printings.

ISBN 9780-76388-754-4 (print)
ISBN 978-0-76388-748-3 (digital)

© 2020 by Paradigm Publishing, LLC
875 Montreal Way
St. Paul, MN 55102
Email: CustomerService@ParadigmEducation.com
Website: ParadigmEducation.com

All rights reserved. No part of this publication may be adapted, reproduced, stored in a retrieval system, or transmitted in any form or by any means, electronic, mechanical, photocopying, recording, or otherwise, without prior written permission from the publisher.

Printed in the United States of America

29 28 27 26 25 24 23 22 21 20   1 2 3 4 5 6 7 8 9 10

Chapter 1	Using Windows 10 and Managing Files	1
Chapter 2	Navigating and Searching the Web	7
Chapter 3	Exploring Office 2019 Essentials	11
Chapter 4	Using OneNote for Windows 10	15
Chapter 5	Communicating and Scheduling Using Outlook	19
Chapter 6	Creating, Editing, and Formatting Word Documents	23
Chapter 7	Enhancing a Word Document with Special Features	29
Chapter 8	Creating, Editing, and Formatting Excel Worksheets	35
Chapter 9	Inserting Functions and Enhancing an Excel Worksheet	41
Chapter 10	Creating, Editing, and Formatting a PowerPoint Presentation	47
Chapter 11	Enhancing a Presentation with Multimedia and Animation Effects	55
Chapter 12	Using and Querying an Access Database	61
Chapter 13	Creating a Table, Form, and Report in Access	67
Chapter 14	Integrating Word, Excel, PowerPoint, and Access Content	73
Chapter 15	Using Office Online and OneDrive	79

Chapter 1
Review and Assessment

The following assessments offer opportunities to apply what you have learned in relevant, real-world situations. Save your solution files and URLs, and submit them for evaluation as directed by your instructor.

Assessment 1.1 Exploring Windows 10 Apps

Type: Individual
Deliverable: Screen Capture of Desktop with Task View
Note: If necessary, insert your USB flash drive into an available USB port on your PC.

1. Start Windows 10 and sign in.
2. Start the News app. Click the link to a story that interests you. Choose an alternative Windows app if the News app is not available on your device.
3. Start the Weather app and view the current weather forecast. Choose an alternative Windows app if the Weather app is not available on your device.
4. Start the Store app. Click the Games tab. Find a free game that looks fun and click the link to read the game description. Choose an alternative Windows app to explore if the Store app is not available on your device.
5. Display Task View.
6. Press the Print Screen key on the keyboard to capture an image of your screen with Task View active. The key may be labeled Prt Sc, PrtScrn, or PrtSc and is generally located in the top row of keys at the right near the last function key. On some PCs or devices, you may need to press Shift + Print Screen or a function key with Print Screen. If you are using a tablet without a keyboard, such as the Microsoft Surface Pro tablet, you can take a screen capture by holding down the Windows key and pressing the Volume Down button. If necessary, check with your instructor for instructions on how to submit assessments with screen capture deliverables.
7. Use the search text box to search for and launch the Paint desktop app.
8. Click the Paste button on the Paint Home tab or insert the screen capture by opening the screen capture if you used a method other than those described in Step 6.
9. Click the Save button on the Quick Access Toolbar at the top of the Paint window. In the Save As dialog box, navigate to your USB flash drive in the left pane, select the current file name in the *File name* text box, type TaskView -YourName, and then click the Save button. (You will move this file to another location in Assessment 1.4.)
10. Close the Paint window.
11. Close each of the three apps you started in this assessment.
12. Submit the assessment to your instructor in the manner requested.

- Glossary
- Infographic
- Crossword Puzzle
- Multiple Choice
- Completion
- Matching
- Assessments
- Chapter Exam

Assessment 1.2 Customizing the Start Menu and Desktop

Type: Individual

Deliverable: Screen Capture with Customized Start Menu Shown on Desktop

Note: Skip steps in this assessment that ask you to customize a tile if the tile is already at the instructed setting. If a tile is not available because the app is not installed on your device, customize any available tile on the Start menu.

1. At the desktop, display the Start menu and then resize the Mail tile smaller.
2. Resize the Photos tile to Large.
3. Resize the Microsoft Edge tile to Wide.
4. Turn the Live Tile feature off the Calendar tile.
5. Turn the Live Tile feature off the Mail tile.
6. Rearrange the Mail, Photos, Microsoft Edge, and Calendar tiles to the top of the *Create* section of tiles in an arrangement that suits you.
7. Resize the Start menu wider and taller than the current menu size and then click on the desktop to hide the menu.
8. Open the Settings app and change the background image for the desktop to another image of your preference.
9. Change the accent color to another color of your preference and then close the Settings window.
10. Display the Start menu and then capture an image of your customized Start menu and desktop. Paste the image into a new Paint window. See Assessment 1.1, Steps 6 to 8 if you need help.
11. Save the image in Paint on your USB flash drive as **Personalization-YourName**.
12. Close the Paint window.
13. Submit the assessment to your instructor in the manner requested.
14. Repeat Steps 1 to 9 to restore the tiles, Start menu, background, and accent color to their original settings and rearrange the tiles back to their original locations.

Assessment 1.3 Browsing Files with File Explorer

Type: Individual

Deliverable: Screen Capture with File Explorer Window

1. Start File Explorer.
2. In the File Explorer window, display in the Content pane the files and folders on your USB flash drive.
3. Navigate the following folders: ComputerCourse, CompletedTopics, Ch1.
4. With the Ch1 files displayed in the Content pane, change the view to *Large icons*.
5. Capture an image of the desktop with the File Explorer window open and paste it into a Paint window.
6. Save the image in Paint on your USB flash drive as **FileExplorer-YourName**.
7. Close the Paint window and then close the File Explorer window.
8. Submit the assessment to your instructor in the manner requested.

Assessment 1.4 Performing File Management Tasks

Type: Individual

Deliverable: Screen Capture with File Explorer Window

1. Start File Explorer and display in the Content pane the Assessments folder on your USB flash drive.
2. Create a new folder named *Ch1*.
3. Display the StudentDataFiles folder in the Content pane and then copy the Ch1 folder to the ComputerCourse folder.

4. Display in the Content pane the Ch1 folder within the ComputerCourse folder.
5. Select all files within the folder and move them to the Ch1 folder within Assessments.
6. With the Content pane displaying the files in the Ch1 folder within Assessments, do the following:
   a. Delete the files named **Fireworks**, **Winter**, and **PaintingBunting**.
   b. Rename the file **MurresOnIce** to *BirdsOnIceFloe*.
   c. Rename the file **BMMF** to *DrumsSolo*.
   d. Create a new folder named *NASA*.
   e. Select and move the following files to the NASA folder: **Apollo11Parade**, **ApolloLanding1966**, **ArmstrongMoon1969**, and **NASA_SpaceXFlight**.
   f. If necessary, change the view to *List*.
7. Capture an image of the desktop with the File Explorer window showing the Content pane for the Ch1 folder within Assessments and paste it into a Paint window.
8. Save the image in Paint on your USB flash drive as **Ch1FileExplorer-YourName**.
9. Close the Paint window.
10. Display in the Content pane the ComputerCourse folder and then delete the folders Ch1 and StudentDataFiles. Click Yes at any messages that appear asking to confirm deletion of files. (Note that another copy of the folder StudentDataFiles is on the USB flash drive.)
11. Create a new folder named *ScreenCaptures* within the Ch1 folder in Assessments. Move all the Paint files from Assessment 1.1 to Step 8 of this assessment to the ScreenCaptures folder.
12. Close the File Explorer window.
13. Submit the assessment (from Step 8) to your instructor in the manner requested.

Assessment 1.5 Planning a New Folder Structure

Type: Individual
Deliverable: Document with Recommended Folder Structure

1. Assume that you volunteer at the local animal rescue organization. You have been asked by the board of directors to organize the files stored on the computer in the office. In looking through the Documents folder in File Explorer, you discover that all the files have been saved to the Documents folder without any structure. In looking through the folder, you determine the following types of files are present:
   - photographs of cats, dogs, horses, and other animals that have been rescued
   - reports and invoices from veterinarians who attended to rescued animals
   - contact information for donors
   - budget and donor financial worksheets
   - applications from adoption families
   - minutes of board meetings
   - fundraising activities
   - supplies lists
   - animal pharmaceuticals
   - individual rescue animal records including adoptee information
2. Create a plan for a folder structure that will allow you to organize the Documents folder so that related files are grouped in a logical manner.

3. Start the WordPad desktop app (find WordPad using the search text box) and create a document that explains your planned folder structure for the animal rescue charity.
4. Click the Save button on the Quick Access Toolbar at the top of the WordPad window. In the Save As dialog box, navigate to the Ch1 folder in Assessments on your USB flash drive, type the file name AnimalRescueFolders-YourName, and then click the Save button.
5. Close the WordPad window.
6. Submit the assessment to your instructor in the manner requested.

Assessment 1.6 Using Microsoft's Virtual Agent to Learn About Timeline Feature

Type: Individual
Deliverable: Document about Windows 10 Timeline Feature

1. Open the Get Help app. This app opens a window where you can type questions about Windows features and the virtual agent replies with help information or links.
2. Type About Timeline in the message text box and then press Enter or click the Send message icon.
3. Read about the Timeline feature in the reply sent by the virtual agent. In particular, learn how to limit the activity history. If necessary, click the link to more help that takes you to a Windows support web page.
4. Start Wordpad (find WordPad using the search text box) and type in a new document screen the main points that you learned about the Timeline feature using your own words (do not copy and paste the information from the app window or web page).
5. Save the WordPad document as **Timeline-YourName** in the Ch1 folder in Assessments on your USB flash drive.
6. Close the WordPad window.
7. Submit the assessment to your instructor in the manner requested.

Assessment 1.7 Go Mobile—Using a File Manager on Your Smartphone

Type: Individual or Pairs
Deliverable: Screenshot from Smartphone and Document

1. Android and Apple devices include a built-in file manager app to view and manage files stored on the device and at connected cloud services. Find the app on your smartphone and review the files that you have stored. Find out the options for managing those files. For example, can you move, rename, and delete files?
2. Take a screenshot of the page that loads when the app is started. (If necessary, search online for the steps to take a screenshot on your smartphone.)
3. If necessary, download the Microsoft Word app to your smartphone from the app store for your device.
4. Launch the Word app and then create a document using point form to describe the name of the file manager app and the tasks you can perform on files using the app.
5. Save the document as **PhoneFileMgt-YourName**. Use a cloud storage service (such as OneDrive) to save the document online so that you have access to the document from another device.
6. Submit the assessment to your instructor in the manner requested.

Assessment 1.8 Job Ready—Finding Resources for Learning Windows 10

Type: Pairs or Teams
Deliverable: Presentation

1. Search at YouTube for videos about learning Windows 10. Use the Filter feature at YouTube's web page to filter the search results to short-duration videos uploaded this year.
2. Watch at least two videos that interest you.
3. Create a presentation that provides a few slides with bulleted lists of key points you learned from the videos you watched.
4. Include links to the videos you watched on the last slide.
5. Save the presentation as **LearnWindows-YourName** in the Ch1 folder in Assessments on your USB flash drive.
6. Submit the assessment to your instructor in the manner requested.

Chapter 2
Review and Assessment

The following assessments offer opportunities to apply what you have learned in relevant, real-world situations. Save your solution files and URLs, and submit them for evaluation as directed by your instructor.

Assessment 2.1 Browsing Web Pages

Type: Individual
Deliverable: Screen Captures of Web Pages or PDF Documents of Web Pages

1. Start Edge or Chrome and navigate to www.nga.gov, which is the web page for the National Gallery of Art in Washington, DC.
2. Navigate to the Current Exhibitions page and then click the hyperlink to a current exhibition of your choosing.
3. Add the page to Favorites (Edge) or bookmark the page (Chrome).
4. Do *one* of the following tasks (check with your instructor for his or her preferred output method):
    a. Save a screen capture of the web page you visited in a file named **WebBrowsing1-YourName** in a new folder named *Ch2* created within the Assessments folder on your storage medium.
    b. Select *Microsoft Print to PDF* as the Printer in the Print dialog box and then click Print. A PDF document is generated from the web page. In the Save Print Output As dialog box, save the PDF document as **WebBrowsing1-YourName** in a new folder named *Ch2* in the Assessments folder on your storage medium.
5. Open a new tab and navigate to www.navy.mil, the web page for the US Navy.
6. Add the page to Favorites (Edge) or bookmark the page (Chrome).
7. Navigate to one of the Navy News Service Top Stories.
8. Save a screen capture of the web page, or print to a PDF document. Use the same method you followed in Step 4 and name the new file **WebBrowsing2-YourName** in the Ch2 folder in Assessments on your storage medium.

- Glossary
- Infographic
- Crossword Puzzle
- Multiple Choice
- Completion
- Matching
- Assessments
- Chapter Exam

9. Close the tab for the National Gallery of Art page.
10. Display the Favorites list in Edge or the Bookmarks bar in Chrome and save a screen capture of the browser window in a file named **WebFavorites-YourName** in the Ch2 folder in Assessments on your storage medium.
11. Close Edge or Chrome and any other applications that you may have opened.
12. Submit the assessment to your instructor in the manner requested.

Assessment 2.2 Searching for Information on the Web

Type: Individual

Deliverable: Document with Search Criteria and Search Results Information

1. Start Edge or Chrome.
2. Display the web page for your favorite search engine and search for information on résumé writing tips.
3. Start a new WordPad document (find WordPad using the search text box) and record the following information:
   a. Record the search engine you used and the search phrase you typed to find information.
   b. Record the number of pages returned in the search results list. *Note: Some search engines show the number of results at the bottom of the first page.*
4. Next, return to the web browser and apply search options at the search engine website to help you narrow the search results. If necessary, use the Help feature for the search engine to learn how to specify advanced search options, or use a different search engine that offers more options for narrowing a search.
5. Switch to the document window and type a description of the search options you applied and the number of pages returned in the new search results list.
6. Switch to the web browser, navigate to one of the hyperlinks on the search results page, and read the information. Select and copy the URL in the Address bar.
7. Switch to the document window, paste the URL of the page you visited below the search statistics, and add in your own words a brief summary in point form of new information you learned by reading the web page.
8. Save the document as **ResumeSearch-YourName** in the Ch2 folder in Assessments on your storage medium.
9. Close the web browser and WordPad windows.
10. Submit the assessment to your instructor in the manner requested.

Assessment 2.3 Downloading Content from a Web Page

Type: Individual

Deliverable: Document with Downloaded Photograph of World War I Soldiers

1. Start Edge or Chrome and navigate to The Commons page at flickr.com. (If necessary, refer to Topic 2.2, Step 19 for the URL.)
2. Search The Commons for images of soldiers from World War I.
3. Select and download an image to your computer.
4. Start a new WordPad document and paste the image into the document. (Use the Picture button on the Home tab.)
5. Switch to the web browser, select and copy the URL for the photograph, and paste it below the image in the document.
6. Save the document as **WWISoldiers-YourName** in the Ch2 folder in Assessments on your storage medium.
7. Close the WordPad and web browser windows.
8. Submit the assessment to your instructor in the manner requested.

Assessment 2.4 Exploring a New Search Engine

Type: Individual or Pairs
Deliverable: Document with Comparison Information for Two Search Engines

1. Start Edge or Chrome, navigate to your favorite search engine web page, and search for information on job interview techniques. Apply advanced search options to try to narrow the search results to high-quality information about job interviews.
2. Next, conduct a search using the phrase *top five search engines*.
3. Read at least one article in the search results. Choose a search engine from the article that you do not normally use. If you are doing this assessment in pairs, each person selects a different search engine.
4. Navigate to the new search engine you selected and conduct a search on job interview techniques. Use the same search phrase at each search engine.
5. Compare the search results from each search engine. Were the number of pages in the search results close to the same number? On page one of search results at each search engine, how many web pages were repeated and how many web pages were different? Did one search engine seem to return more targeted results? Do you think you will use the new search engine in the future, or will you revert to the one you favored before?
6. Create a WordPad document with answers to the questions and, for the last question, provide your reasons. Include the two search engines and the search phrase you used to complete this assessment.
7. Save the document as **SearchEngineComparison-YourName** in the Ch2 folder in Assessments on your storage medium.
8. Close the WordPad and web browser windows.
9. Submit the assessment to your instructor in the manner requested.

Assessment 2.5 Exploring Creative Commons Content

Type: Individual or Pairs
Deliverable: Document with Information on Creative Commons Licenses and Content

1. Start Edge or Chrome and navigate to creativecommons.org.
2. Click What we do, read the information that describes Creative Commons, and then click Learn more about our programs and read the mission and vision information.
3. Click Search the Commons (at the top of the page) and find an image of a well-known landmark in your geographic area available under a creative commons license using any of the search services provided.
4. Download a copy of the image and insert the image into a WordPad document. Copy and paste the URL for the image below the photograph.
5. Add a brief summary in your own words below the image of the main points from the information you read about Creative Commons.
6. Save the document as **CreativeCommons-YourName** in the Ch2 folder in Assessments on your storage medium.
7. Close the WordPad and web browser windows.
8. Submit the assessment to your instructor in the manner requested.

Mobile

Assessment 2.6 Go Mobile—Searching On The Go

Type: Individuals
Deliverable: Screenshot from Smartphone

1. Use the mobile browser on your smartphone to navigate to the website for your school.
2. Search your school website for the career services department page. Find information about the support services offered to help students find employment. If your school offers a job posting service for employers looking to hire students, click a hyperlink to a job posting that interests you.
3. Take a screenshot of the page with the information you viewed at Step 2.
4. Submit the screenshot to your instructor in the manner requested.

Jobs

Assessment 2.7 Job Ready—Submitting Electronic Job Applications

Type: Individual, Pairs, or Teams
Deliverable: Presentation

1. Search for articles that provide best practices for formatting and submitting electronic job applications. Use search tools to narrow the search results to articles written in the past year.
2. Select and read two articles in the search results list.
3. Create a presentation with a minimum of five slides that provides a summary of the main points in both articles.
4. Include a sixth slide with the URLs of the articles you read.
5. Save the presentation as **ElectronicJobApps-YourName** in the Ch2 folder in Assessments on your storage medium.
6. Submit the assessment to your instructor in the manner requested.

The following assessments offer opportunities to apply what you have learned in relevant, real-world situations. Save your solution files and URLs, and submit them for evaluation as directed by your instructor.

- Glossary
- Infographic
- Crossword Puzzle
- Multiple Choice
- Completion
- Matching
- Assessments
- Exercises
- Projects
- Skills Exam
- Chapter Exam

Assessment 3.1 Start a New Presentation and Copy Object to Slide from Excel

Type: Individual
Deliverable: PowerPoint Presentation

1. Start Excel and then open the student data file named **CutRateRentals**.
2. Start a new blank presentation in PowerPoint.
3. Type CutRate Car Rentals as the slide title text.
4. Click the Layout button in the Slides group on the Home tab and then click *Title Only* to change the slide layout. If the Design Ideas task pane opens at the right, close the pane.
5. Select the title text, apply bold and italic formatting, change the color of the text to a color of your choice, and then deselect the text.
6. Switch to Excel, select and copy the pie chart, switch to PowerPoint, and then paste the chart on the slide.
7. Save the presentation as **CutRateRentals-YourName** in a new folder named *Ch3* in the Assessments folder in the location requested by your instructor.
8. Close PowerPoint and then close Excel.
9. Submit the assessment to your instructor in the manner requested.

Assessment 3.2 Modify a Presentation and Copy Content to Word

Type: Individual
Deliverable: Word Document and PDF Document

1. Start PowerPoint and then open the **CutRateRentals-YourName** presentation.
2. Use Save As to save a copy of the file in the same location as **CutRateRentalsRevised-YourName**.
3. Select and resize the chart using a corner selection handle so the chart fills most of the slide below the title.
4. With the chart still selected, move it as needed so that it is centered on the slide horizontally using the center alignment guide to assist you with the move. *Hint: Do not drag to move the chart while the mouse is positioned over a pie slice.*
5. With the chart still selected, use the Change Colors gallery in the Chart Styles group on the Chart Tools Design tab to change the color scheme for the pie chart to another color palette of your choosing.

6. With the chart still selected, use the Shape Styles gallery on the Chart Tools Format tab to apply a shape style option of your choosing. *Hint: Click the More button (bottom button that displays with a bar and down-pointing arrow below it at the right end of the gallery) to view more options in a drop-down grid.*
7. Save the revised presentation using the same name.
8. Start a new blank document in Word.
9. Copy the slide title text from the PowerPoint presentation and paste the text into the Word document. After the text is pasted, use the Paste Options button to apply the *Keep Source Formatting* option.
10. Press Enter to create a new blank line after the title text.
11. Copy the chart from the PowerPoint presentation and paste it below the title in the Word document.
12. Save the Word document as **CutRateRentals-YourName** in the Ch3 folder in Assessments in the location requested by your instructor.
13. Export the Word document as a PDF with the same name and save in the same Ch3 folder as Step 12.
14. If a window opens with the PDF document in it, close the window.
15. Close Word and then close PowerPoint.
16. Submit the assessment to your instructor in the manner requested.

Visual — Assessment 3.3 Visual—Create a Florida Vacation Flyer

Type: Individual or Pairs
Deliverable: Flyer as Document or PDF

1. Research a Florida destination that you would like to travel to during the next school break, including the approximate cost for one week. Include in the cost estimate travel, lodging, food, visitor attractions, and souvenirs.
2. Make a list of 5 to 10 points to include in the flyer based on the research you conducted. For example, provide a list of tourist attractions or events that make the destination inviting.
3. Create a flyer in Word named **FloridaFlyer-YourName** similar to Assessment 3.3 Florida Vacation Flyer shown on the next page and save it in the Ch3 folder in Assessments in the location requested by your instructor. Substitute information from your research in place of the example text. Use your best judgment to determine formatting options to apply to the text. Apply the following options to the picture: Brightness +20% Contrast +40% correction, width of 3.5 inches, Top and Bottom Text Wrapping, and Reflected Rounded Rectangle Picture Style.
4. Export the flyer as a PDF with the same name, save in the same location, and then close Word.
5. Submit the assessment to your instructor in the manner requested.

Florida Vacation

Are you ready for a week of fun and adventure?

Read on to learn about a fantastic Florida vacation.

When: Dec. 21st-Dec. 31st, 20xx

Where: Sarasota, Florida

Reasons not to miss this trip:
- Ringling Museum of Art
- Marie Selby Botanical Gardens
- Myakka River State Park
- Historic Spanish Point
- Big Cat Habitat and Gulf Coast Sanctuary
- Mote Marine Aquarium
- Sarasota Bay Explorers
- G.WIZ- The Science Museum

Estimated Cost: $1755.00 per person based on one week.

Assessment 3.3 Florida Vacation Flyer

Assessment 3.4 Use Tell Me to Find Help on a PowerPoint Feature

Type: Individual
Deliverable: PowerPoint Presentation

1. Start PowerPoint and then open the file **CutRateRentals-YourName** created in Assessment 3.1.
2. Use Save As to save a copy of the file in the same location as **CutRateRentalsBar-YourName**.
3. Use the Tell Me feature to help you change the chart from a 3-D pie chart to a 3-D Clustered Bar chart.
4. Resize the bar chart so that it fills up as much of the slide as possible below the title.
5. Save the revised presentation using the same name and then close PowerPoint.
6. Submit the assessment to your instructor in the manner requested.

Assessment 3.5 Go Mobile—Creating a Document on the Go

Type: Individual
Deliverable: Word Document

1. If necessary, download the Word mobile app to your smartphone.
2. Take a photo using the camera on your smartphone of the front of your school or a building nearby if you are taking this course online.
3. Start a new blank document using the Word app on your smartphone. Type the title of your school at the top of the document. On the next line, type a brief description of the building that you took a photo of in Step 2 (such as *Main Entrance*) and then press Enter.
4. Insert the image you took in Step 2 on the blank line below the building description.
5. Add at least two sentences below the image that explain the program you are registered in and the reason you decided to attend your school.
6. Press Enter twice after the text typed in Step 5 and then type your name.
7. Use Save As to change the document name to **MySchool-YourName**, saving it in your OneDrive personal storage account or in the location requested by your instructor.
8. Submit the document to your instructor in the manner requested.

Assessment 3.6 Job Ready—Using the Dictation Feature

Type: Individual, Pairs, or Teams
Deliverable: Document or Presentation

Windows 10 includes a Dication toolbar that can be activated at any time to dictate text in any application instead of typing. The dictation feature may help you enter and edit text into an Office application more efficiently, but the feature requires some practice to get used to the way to speak commands.

1. Navigate to the support website for Windows by typing the URL https://support.microsoft.com in a browser Address bar.
2. Use the search text box on the Microsoft Support website to find information on the dictation feature included with Windows 10, including dictation commands.
3. Open a blank Word document and practice the dictation feature by dictating at least two paragraphs that explain the plot in a recent movie you saw or a book that you read.
4. Create a document or a presentation that explains how to use the dictation feature. Provide the instruction for what to say to insert five commonly used symbols. Include a paragraph at the end of the document that describes your experience with dictating in Step 3 by answering these questions:
   • Did the feature allow you to enter text more efficiently?
   • Did the feature correctly interpret your spoken words?
   • Were there any commands that were incorrectly interpreted by the feature?
   • Will you use this feature when creating a document at work? Why or why not?
5. Add the URL for the article you used from the Microsoft Support website that provided the information for this assessment.
6. Save the document or presentation as **Dictation-YourName** in the Ch3 folder in Assessments in the location requested by your instructor.
7. Submit the assessment to your instructor in the manner requested.

OneNote for Windows 10 — Chapter 4 Review and Assessment

The following assessments offer opportunities to apply what you have learned in relevant, real-world situations. Save your solution files and URLs, and submit them for evaluation as directed by your instructor.

Assessment 4.1 Start a New Notebook and Create Notebook Structure

Type: Individual
Deliverable: OneNote Notebook (Continued in Assessment 4.2)

1. Start OneNote and display the Notebooks list. Create a new notebook named **NotebookPractice-YourName**, and then close the Notebook pane.
2. Rename New Section 1 section tab *Computer Research* and add page title *Images*.
3. Add a new section titled *Law Course* with a page titled *Current Topics in Law*.
4. Add a new section titled *Tourism Course* with a page titled *Presentations*.
5. Add a new section titled *Volunteer Work* with a page titled *Medical Clinic Association Conference*.
6. Leave the notebook open for Assessment 4.2; otherwise, close OneNote.

Assessment 4.2 Adding Notes and External Content to a Notebook

Type: Individual
Deliverable: OneNote Notebook (Continued from Assessment 4.1 and continues in Assessment 4.3)

1. If necessary, start OneNote.
2. Embed a PDF copy of the file **MedClinicsFees** on the Medical Clinic Association Conference page in the Volunteer Work section.
3. Embed a PDF copy of the presentation **WaikikiPres** on the Presentations page in the Tourism Course section.
4. Attach the Word document **FamilyAndLawAssgnt** as a file on the Current Topics in Law page in the Law Course section and type Assignment 1 due in week 5 as note text with the icon.
5. Insert image **IBMCptr_1961.jpg** on the Images page in the Computer Research section and type IBM computer from 1961 as note text below the photograph.
6. Add a new page to the Computer Research section with the page title *History of Computers* and add a hyperlink to the web address https://www.computerhistory.org/timeline. Type The Timeline of Computer History from the Computer History Museum provides the history of computing starting in 1933 and continuing to present day as note text below the hyperlink.
7. Leave the notebook open if you are continuing on to Assessment 4.3; otherwise, close OneNote.

Sidebar:
- Glossary
- Infographic
- Crossword Puzzle
- Multiple Choice
- Completion
- Matching
- Assessments
- Chapter Exam

Assessment 4.3 Tagging Notes, Adding a Copy of a Web Page, and Sharing a Notebook

Type: Individual
Deliverable: Shared OneNote Notebook and PDF of Notebook (Continued from Assessments 4.1 and 4.2)

1. If necessary, start OneNote.
2. Assign the To-Do tag at the beginning of the note text with the Word document icon on the Current Topics in Law page in the Law Course section.
3. Add the Important tag at the top of the slides embedded on the Presentations page in the Tourism Course section and type This is included in test 1 as note text with the tag.
4. Open a browser window and search for a recent article about 3-D printing technology. Copy and paste the article title and the first few paragraphs to a new page in the Computer Research section titled *3-D Printing*. Add an Important tag above the copied content and type Article for project 1 as note text with the tag. Close the browser window when finished.
5. Click the Settings and More button (displays as three dots) near the top right corner of the window and click *Print*. In the Print dialog box, change the following options:
   - Change the *Printer* option to *Microsoft Print to PDF*
   - Change the *Orientation* option to *Landscape*
   - Change the *Pages* option to *Current Notebook*

   Click Print, navigate to the Assessments folder on your storage medium, and create a new folder *Ch4*. Double-click to open the Ch4 folder, type NotebookPractice-YourName in the *file name* text box, and then click Save.
6. Share the notebook with your instructor if instructed to do so.
7. Submit the assessment to your instructor in the manner requested.

Assessment 4.4 Creating a Notebook Repository for Assessments

Type: Individual
Deliverable: Shared Notebook on OneDrive

Note: Check with your instructor before completing this assessment. Your instructor may not want you to share the notebook.

1. Create a new notebook with the name **MyAssessments-YourName**.
2. Rename the New Section 1 section tab *Windows* and add the page title *Chapter 1*.
3. Add the following sections and enter the page titles given for the Internet, Office, and OneNote sections.

Sections	Pages
Internet	Chapter 2
Office	Chapter 3
OneNote	Chapter 4
Outlook	
Word	
Excel	
PowerPoint	
Access	
Integrating	
OneDrive	

4. Make the Chapter 1 page in the Windows section active and then insert a copy of the first assessment file that you completed for Chapter 1. Next, insert a copy

of each remaining assessment file for Chapter 1 in the order completed, one below the other. Review each file on your storage medium before inserting it to determine if you should add the file to the page using the File button, the PDF button, or the Pictures button (screen captures or other images).
5. Make the Chapter 2 page in the Internet section active and repeat the process you completed in Step 4 to insert a copy of each assessment file that you completed for Chapter 2.
6. Make the Chapter 3 page in the Office section active and repeat the process you completed in Step 4 to insert a copy of each assessment file that you completed for Chapter 3.
7. Make the Chapter 4 page in the OneNote section active and insert a copy of the PDF file created for Assessment 4.3.
8. Share the notebook with your instructor.
9. Close OneNote.

Assessment 4.5 Go Mobile—A City To Visit

Type: Individual
Deliverable: Email Message with PDF File Attachment

1. If necessary, download the OneNote mobile app to your smartphone.
2. Using the mobile browser on your device, find an article about a city that you would like to visit. Find interesting facts, history, or other information about the city of interest to you.
3. Copy the URL of the article you read to the clipboard or clip tray on your smartphone.
4. Start the OneNote mobile app and add a new page with an appropriate title.
5. Paste the URL from Step 3 on the new page.
6. Below the hyperlink, type five points that you learned about the city from the article.
7. In the OneNote app, tap the menu button (three vertical dots) and tap *Share page*, then tap *PDF* when prompted in the Share As box. Send the PDF as an email message to your instructor with an appropriate message and subject line, or otherwise submit the assessment to your instructor in the manner requested.

Assessment 4.7 Job Ready—Managing a Shared Notebook

Type: Individual, Pairs, or Teams
Deliverable: Document or Presentation

Once a OneNote notebook is shared, anyone can edit any content on any page. Clear guidelines should be in place for making changes to shared content to avoid someone changing someone else's work without the original author's knowledge.

1. Research the option in OneNote to protect a section with a password.
2. Discuss within your group whether protecting sections with a password would be a good option to manage changes made by multiple editors in a shared notebook. What other options, including non-technology solutions, should a group adopt to avoid someone changing someone else's work?
3. Create a document or a presentation that summarizes the information you learned about protecting sections with a password and a point form summary of your team's discussion.
4. Save the document or presentation as **ShareEtiquette-YourName** in the Ch4 folder in Assessments on your storage medium.
5. Submit the assessment to your instructor in the manner requested.

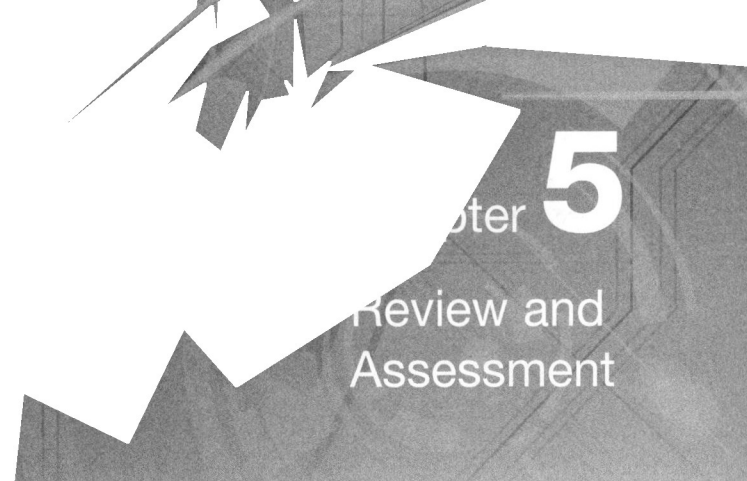

Chapter 5 Review and Assessment

The following assessments offer opportunities to apply what you have learned in relevant, real-world situations. Save your solution files and URLs, and submit them for evaluation as directed by your instructor.

Assessment 5.1 Open an Outlook Data File and Add and Edit Items

Type: Individual
Deliverable: Updated Outlook Data File (Continued in Assessment 5.2)

1. Create a new folder named *Ch5* in the Assessments folder on your storage medium.
2. Start Outlook.
3. Open an existing Outlook data file with Outlook items by completing the following steps:
   a. Click the File tab and then click *Open & Export*.
   b. Click the Open Outlook Data File button in the Open backstage area.
   c. In the Open Outlook Data File dialog box, navigate to the Ch5 folder in StudentDataFiles on your storage medium and then double-click the file **Ch5-OutlookPracticeData**. A new entry appears in the Folder pane below your current mail folders. The entry may be labeled *Outlook Data File* or *Ch5-OutlookPracticeData*.
4. Click the white right-pointing arrow next to the new entry *Outlook Data File* or *Ch5-OutlookPracticeData* in the Folder pane to expand the folder list. Click the black diagonal downward-pointing arrow next to your email address (or your Outlook user name) in the Folder pane to collapse the folder list. The Folder pane should now show only the mail folders below the new data file opened in Step 3 along with your email address (at the top).

Note: For the remaining steps in this assessment and the next assessment, complete all tasks using the folders in the expanded folder list for the data file you opened in Step 3.

5. Make Inbox active to view the two messages, and forward each message to yourself (use your email address) with the message text *Here is a copy of the message from [enter sender's name in the original message]*.
6. Display all the other folders in the data file by clicking the More button (displays as three dots) on the Navigation pane and then clicking *Folders* in the pop-up list. Collapse again the list of folders for your regular email account.

- Glossary
- Infographic
- Crossword Puzzle
- Multiple Choice
- Completion
- Matching
- Assessments
- Chapter Exam

7. Click *Calendar* in the Folder pane and display October 11, 2021 in the Appointment area. Make the following changes to appointments in the Calendar (respond Yes to any messages that appear about reminders):
    a. On Monday, October 11, add *Room A-109* as the location for the *Project updates* appointment.
    b. Change the lunch with Taylor Gorski from Tuesday, October 12 to Wednesday, October 13 at 1:00 p.m.
    c. Make the doctor appointment on Wednesday, October 13, 1.5 hours in duration.
    d. Change the *Health and Safety Training* on October 14 to Friday, October 15 and make it a recurring appointment at the same day and time for three weeks.
8. Click *Contacts* in the Folder pane and make the following changes to the People list:
    a. Change the *Work* telephone number for Xavier Borman to *888-555-4523*.
    b. Change the *Title* for Taylor Gorski to *President & CEO*.
    c. Add a new person to the People list with the following contact information and add a picture using the file **LuisPhillips** in the Ch5 folder in StudentDataFiles:
        Luis Phillips, NewAge Advertising, Sales Representative, luis@ppi-edu.net
9. Click *Tasks* in the Folder pane and make the following changes:
    a. Remove the task *Find volunteers to help at conference* from the To-Do List.
    b. Mark the task *Update project wiki pages* completed.
    c. Change the due date for the task *Research click marketing strategies* to October 22, 2021.
    d. Add the following new tasks:
        Compile report from volunteer survey
        Return equipment rented for conference
10. Leave Outlook open if you are continuing to Assessment 5.2; otherwise, right-click **Outlook Data File** or **Ch5-OutlookPracticeData** and then click the *Close* option (e.g. *Close "Outlook Data File"*). Close Outlook and submit the assessment to your instructor in the manner requested.

Assessment 5.2 Sending Outlook Items to a OneNote Notebook and Creating a PDF

Type: Individual
Deliverable: Page in OneNote Notebook and PDFs for Outlook Items in Assessment 5.1

Note: You must have completed Assessment 4.4 in Chapter 4 and Assessment 5.1 in this chapter before starting this assessment.

1. Start OneNote. With the MyAssessments notebook active, click the Outlook section tab and then type *Chapter 5* as the page title.
2. Switch to Outlook and make Calendar active. Display October 11, 2021 in the Appointment area and send the calendar to your OneNote notebook by completing the following steps:
    a. Click the Month button in the Arrange group on the Home tab if the calendar is not displayed in Month view.
    b. Display the Print backstage area and change the printer to *Microsoft Print to PDF*.
    c. Click the Print button.
    d. In the Save Print Output As dialog box, navigate to the Ch5 folder in Assessments on your storage medium, type *Calendar-YourName* in the *File name* text box, and then click Save.

3. Display the Contacts folder. Display the Print backstage area and print the People list in *Card Style* using the Microsoft Print to PDF printer, saving as **PeopleList-YourName** in the Ch5 folder in Assessments.
4. Display the Tasks folder. Change the current view to Simple List. Display the Print backstage area and print the task list in *Table Style* using the Microsoft Print to PDF printer, saving as **TaskList-YourName** in the Ch5 folder in Assessments.
5. Display Mail. Right-click *Outlook Data File* or *Ch5-OutlookPracticeData* in the Folder pane and then click the *Close* option (e.g. *Close "Outlook Data File"*).
6. If necessary, expand the folder list for your email account by clicking the white right-pointing arrow.
7. If necessary, make Inbox the active folder and update the message list.
8. Open the first message window for the message you forwarded to yourself in Assessment 5.1, Step 5. Display the Print backstage area and print the message, saving it as **Message1-YourName** in the Ch5 folder in Assessments.
9. Repeat Step 8 for the second message you forwarded to yourself in Assessment 5.1, Step 5, saving the second message as **Message2-YourName** in the Ch5 folder in Assessments.
10. Switch to OneNote. Insert each PDF printout created from Steps 2 to 9 one below the other.
11. Leave OneNote open if you are continuing to Assessment 5.3; otherwise, close OneNote.
12. In Outlook, click *Mail* on the Navigation pane to restore the Folder pane to the default folder list that displays mail folders only.
13. Leave Outlook open if you are continuing to Assessment 5.3; otherwise, close Outlook and submit the assessment to your instructor in the manner requested.

Assessment 5.3 Organizing Your School Activities in Outlook

Type: Individual
Deliverable: Page in OneNote Notebook and PDFs for Outlook Items

1. In OneNote, create a new page in the Outlook section with the title *Assessment 5.3*.
2. Switch to Outlook, make Calendar active, and make sure the current date is displayed. Create appointments for your class schedule for all the courses you are currently taking as recurring appointments in the calendar for the remainder of the current semester.
3. Add other appointments to your Outlook calendar for any other school activities that you want to attend. For example, add an appointment or event for any extracurricular school activity. Print the calendar for the current month as a PDF, saving it as **MySchoolCalendar-YourName**.
4. Make People active and add your teacher's contact information to the People list. Print the People list as a PDF, saving it as **MyPeopleList-YourName**.
5. Make Tasks active and create in the To-Do List a task entry for each upcoming test, project, or assignment (including due dates) of which you are aware in each of the courses you are currently taking. Print the To-Do List as a PDF, saving it as **MyTo-DoList-YourName**.
6. Switch to OneNote. Insert each PDF created in this assessment in the order completed on the Assessment 5.3 page in the Outlook section.
7. Close OneNote.
8. Close Outlook.
9. Submit the assessment to your instructor in the manner requested.

Assessment 5.4 Go Mobile—Email Etiquette Guidelines

Type: Individual
Deliverable: Email Message with Image Attachment

1. If necessary, download the Outlook mobile app to your smartphone.
2. Using the mobile browser on your device, find and read at least two articles with information about email etiquette guidelines for the workplace.
3. Take a screenshot on your smartphone of the first page of the article you decide to use as the basis for five tips you will write in the next step.
4. Using the Outlook mobile app, compose an email message to your instructor that provides, in point form, the five tips you will practice when you use email at your job.
5. Attach the screenshot from Step 3 to the message.
6. Send the message or otherwise submit the assessment to your instructor in the manner requested.

Assessment 5.5 Job Ready—Email Retention Policy

Type: Individual, Pairs, or Teams
Deliverable: Document or Presentation

Business is often conducted via email messages between employees, vendors, customers, or other stakeholders of the organization; and email messages can be used as evidence in litigation cases. For these reasons, retention of email messages on the company server is important.

1. Search for information on email retention policies for businesses. Read at least two articles that discuss the issues involved in balancing the need to meet legal requirements for email record retention while avoiding the cost, storage, and labor of saving every email message. What role does each employee fulfill in ensuring information that needs to be retained is secure?
2. Create a document or a presentation that summarizes the information you learned, in point form. Include the URLs for the articles you read.
3. Save the document or presentation as **EmailRetention-YourName** in the Ch5 folder in Assessments on your storage medium.
4. Submit the assessment to your instructor in the manner requested.

Chapter 6
Review and Assessment

The following assessments offer opportunities to apply what you have learned in relevant, real-world situations. Save your solution files and URLs, and submit them for evaluation as directed by your instructor.

Assessment 6.1 Creating, Editing, and Completing a Spelling and Grammar Check in a New Document

Type: Individual
Deliverable: Word Document (Continued in Assessment 6.2)

1. In a new blank document, type the following text, pressing Enter only where indicated.
   Social Media Popularity, Profitability, and Privacy [press Enter]
   Ninety-six percent of Americans and Canadians between the ages of 16 and 24 are internet users. For most people, a majority of time spent on the internet involves the use of social communication websites, such as Facebook. All ages prefer the convenience and accessibility of social media websites to connect with family, friends, and acquaintances. [press Enter]
   Social media websites, such as Facebook, make money using a traditional model of selling advertisements, such as banner and pop-up ads. Facebook games, such as Candy Crush Saga, also provide a source of income for Facebook. [press Enter]
   Users of social media websites such as Facebook need to be wary of privacy issues and security threats. The risk of identity theft, clickjacking, and phishing scams is rising due to the popularity of social media. Review privacy options and keep personal information that could identify you to a stranger to a minimum at each social network. Consider asking your family and friends not to tag you in pictures without your knowledge. [press Enter]
   Your Name [press Enter]
2. Save the document as **SocialMedia-YourName** in a new folder named *Ch6* within the Assessments folder on your storage medium.
3. Edit the document as follows:
   a. In the first sentence, change *16 and 24 are internet users* to *10 and 34 are social media users*.
   b. In the second sentence, change *social communication websites* to *social networking websites*.
   c. Add the following sentence to the end of the second paragraph.
      Revenue from mobile ads represented more than two-thirds of all Facebook advertising income in a recent year.

- Glossary
- Infographic
- Crossword Puzzle
- Multiple Choice
- Completion
- Matching
- Assessments
- Exercises
- Projects
- Skills Exam
- Chapter Exam

d. Delete the last sentence in the first paragraph (it begins with *All ages prefer*).
e. Delete the second sentence in the second paragraph (it begins with *Facebook games*).
f. Move the last sentence in the third paragraph (it begins with *Consider asking*) to the beginning of the last paragraph (before the sentence that begins *Users of social media websites*).
g. Type the following new paragraph after the third paragraph and before your name.
   When posting content at a social media website, be mindful not to violate copyright by copying pictures that belong to someone else. Look for a copyright symbol © or refer to terms of use before downloading content. Be careful also not to misrepresent or misuse a registered trademark of a company. Look for the ® or ™ symbol to identify a company's trademark.
h. Replace all occurrences of *social media* with *social networking*. When finished, change *networking* in the title to *Networking*.
4. Complete a spelling and grammar check of the document.
5. Proofread the document carefully to make sure the document is error-free.
6. Save the revised document using the same name (**SocialMedia-YourName**).
7. Leave the document open if you are continuing to Assessment 6.2; otherwise, close the document and submit the assessment to your instructor in the manner requested.

Assessment 6.2 Editing and Formatting a Document

Type: Individual
Deliverable: Word Document

Note: You must have completed Assessment 6.1 before starting this assessment.

1. If necessary, open **SocialMedia-YourName**.
2. Use Save As to change the file name to **SocialMediaFormatted-YourName**, saving in the same folder.
3. Type the following new paragraph and bulleted list between the second and third paragraphs.
   Facebook's $12.5 billion revenue from a recent year is segmented as follows:
   - 85 percent from ads (including mobile ads)
   - 14 percent from games (such as Candy Crush Saga)
   - 1 percent from other sources
4. Format the document as follows:
   a. Change the title to 12-point Verdana bold red font and center-aligned.
   b. Indent the first line of each paragraph.
   c. Justify the first two and the last two paragraphs.
   d. Select the entire document, change the line spacing to 1.5, and remove the space after paragraphs.
5. Depending on the method used to format a paragraph with a first line indent, the indent position for the last three paragraphs may be at 0.25 inch instead of the 0.5 inch in the first two paragraphs. This occurs because the bulleted list formatting carries over to the paragraphs before and after. If necessary, change the first line indent position to 0.5 inch for the last three paragraphs by positioning the insertion point within the paragraph, opening the Paragraph dialog box, and changing the value in the *By* text box in the *Indentation* section.
6. Save the revised document using the same name (**SocialMediaFormatted-YourName**).
7. Submit the assessment to your instructor in the manner requested.
8. Close the document.

Assessment 6.3 Formatting with Styles

Type: Individual
Deliverable: Word Document

Note: You must have completed Assessment 6.1 before starting this assessment.
1. Open **SocialMedia-YourName**.
2. Use Save As to change the file name to **SocialMediaStyles-YourName**, saving in the same folder.
3. Apply the Heading 1 style to the document title.
4. Select all the text below the title except for your name at the bottom of the document and apply the Emphasis style.
5. Select your name at the bottom of the document and apply the Intense Reference style.
6. Change the Style Set to *Black & White (Classic)*.
7. Save the revised document using the same name (**SocialMediaStyles-YourName**).
8. Submit the assessment to your instructor in the manner requested.
9. Close the document.

Assessment 6.4 Creating an Invoice from a Template

Type: Individual
Deliverable: Invoice Document from Template

1. Search for and select a service invoice template of your choosing to create a new document. Note that you may need to modify the presentation of the information given in Step 3a to match the template you select. For example, not all service invoice templates provide a column for entering a quantity or unit price, but you can type that information in a description column if needed.
2. Personalize the template by adding your name as the company name and your school's address, city, state, ZIP code, and phone as the company information. Fill in other company or invoice information with fictitious information, if necessary.
3. Using today's date, create invoice *136* to:

    Leslie Taylor
    HBC Enterprises
    1240 7th Street West
    St. Paul, MN 55102
    888-555-6954
    taylor@ppi-edu.net

    a. Type the body of the invoice using the following information:

Qty	Description	Unit Price	Total
5 hours	Social media consulting	65.00	325.00

    b. Add or delete other information as needed so the invoice is of mailable quality and does not have any placeholders with missing information.
4. Save the document in the Ch6 folder within the Assessments folder on your storage medium as **InvoiceTemplate-YourName**.
5. Submit the assessment to your instructor in the manner requested.
6. Close the document.

Assessment 6.5 Visual—Campus Flyer from Template

Type: Individual
Deliverable: Campus Flyer

1. Create a flyer for your school campus similar to the one shown in the Assessment 6.5 Campus Flyer below. Use a current date and a location suitable for concerts on or near your campus. Add current popular band names to the *FEATURING* section. Enter a fictitious web address and sponsor information. Make any other changes you think are necessary.

Note: *Search for the template shown using the search phrase* simple flyer *in the New backstage area.*

2. Save the flyer in the Ch6 folder within the Assessments folder on your storage medium as **CampusBandFlyer-YourName**.
3. Submit the assessment to your instructor in the manner requested.
4. Close the document.

CAMPUS BAND BATTLE

WHEN
June 5, 2021
8pm – 12pm

WHERE
Student Union Auditorium
1234 Academic Circle, Berkeley, CA

FEATURING · Your Band Name · Your Band Name · Your Band Name · Your Band Name · Your Band Name · Your Band Name

WEB ADDRESS

ALL AGES EVENT

ADVANCE TICKETS
$18 General
$36 VIP
Group rates available on site

AT THE DOOR
$20 General
$40 VIP
Group rates available on site

SPONSORS
Adventure Works
Alpine Ski House
Contoso, Ltd.
Fourth Coffee
Margie's Travel
School of Fine Art
The Phone Company
Wingtip Toys

BENEFITING
The School of Music and the University Arts and Entertainment Council

Assessment 6.5 Campus Flyer

Assessment 6.6 Audio—Internet Research and Composing a New Document

Type: Individual or Pairs
Deliverable: Word Document

You are asked to help with a project on social media by creating a document that describes what you read online after researching two to three recent events where social media was used to promote social good. The project manager has left you a voicemail with information about the project.

1. Listen to the audio file **SocialMediaForSocialGood_instructions**.
2. Complete the research and compose the document as instructed.
3. Save the document in the Ch6 folder within the Assessments folder on your storage medium as **SocialMediaResearch-YourName**.
4. Submit the assessment to your instructor in the manner requested.
5. Close the document.

Assessment 6.7 Go Mobile—Creating a Document with Conference Locations

Type: Individual
Deliverable: Word Document

1. Open the Word mobile app on your smartphone and start a new blank document.
2. Type today's date and then press Enter to move down to the next line.
3. Type Conference Venue Ideas and then press Enter to move down to the next line.
4. In a bulleted list, type four locations near you that are suitable for hosting a conference attended by approximately 150 people.
5. Press Enter twice after the text typed at Step 4 and then type your name.
6. Use Save As to change the document name to **ConferenceLocations-YourName**, saving it in your OneDrive personal storage account.
7. Submit the assessment to your instructor in the manner requested.
8. Exit the Word mobile app.

Assessment 6.8 Job Ready—Composing a Letter

Type: Individual, Pairs, or Teams
Deliverable: Document

You are a member of a conference planning team organizing a conference to be held next year during the week after the winter semester ends. The conference will be attended by student leaders from all the community colleges in your state or province. The focus of the conference is to learn about current trends in online learning. Your task is to help the committee responsible for choosing the keynote speaker for the conference opening night dinner.

1. The chair of the committee wants you to draft the invitation letter to be sent to the person the committee chooses to invite to be the keynote speaker. Begin by searching online for sample text for a keynote speaker invitation.
2. In a new blank document, type a sample invitation letter with details about your conference. Insert a fictitious name and address for the letter recipient. Include your name in the letter as the writer.
3. Apply font and paragraph format options appropriate for a business letter.
4. Save the document as **SpeakerInvitationLtr-YourName** in the Ch6 folder in Assessments on your storage medium.
5. Submit the assessment to your instructor in the manner requested.

Assessment 6.9 Sending Assessment Work to OneNote Notebook

Type: Individual
Deliverable: New Page in Shared OneNote Notebook

1. Start OneNote and open the MyAssessments notebook created in Chapter 4, Assessment 4.4.
2. Make Word the active section and then type Chapter 6 Assessments as the page title.
3. Switch to Microsoft Word. For each assessment that you completed, open the document, use the *Export* option on the File tab to create a PDF of the document (using the default options), and then close the document. Switch back to OneNote. On the Chapter 6 Assessments page in the Word section in the MyAssessments notebook, insert each PDF printout in order of completion.
4. Close OneNote.
5. Close Word.
6. Submit the assessment to your instructor in the manner requested.

Chapter 7 Review and Assessment

The following assessments offer opportunities to apply what you have learned in relevant, real-world situations. Save your solution files and URLs, and submit them for evaluation as directed by your instructor.

Assessment 7.1 Enhancing a Document with Visual Elements

Type: Individual
Deliverable: National Park Trip Planner Document (Continued in Assessment 7.2)

1. Open **GrandCanyonPlanner**. If necessary, click the Enable Editing button to close Protected view.
2. Save the document as **GrandCanyonPlanner-YourName** in a new folder named *Ch7* within the Assessments folder on your storage medium.
3. Insert, label, and edit images as follows:
   a. Insert the image from the file named ***ScorpionRidge.jpg*** at the right margin aligned with the first line of text in the first paragraph and with the *Square* text wrapping option. Choose an appropriate image size for the image.
   b. Insert the image from the file named ***BrightAngelPoint.jpg*** at the left margin aligned with the first line of text in the last paragraph and with the *Square* text wrapping option. Do *not* resize the image.
   c. Add a caption below the image inserted at Step 3a with the label text *Scorpion Ridge, North Rim*. Accept all default caption options.
   d. Add a caption below the image inserted at Step 3b with the label text *Bright Angel Point, North Rim*. Accept all default caption options.
   e. Apply Picture Styles of your choosing to both images.
   f. Apply Color Saturation at 200% to both images.
4. Add borders, shading, and a text box as follows:
   a. Select the third sentence (begins *Admission to . . .*) in the second paragraph (below subtitle *Park Entrance Fees*), center text, and add an outside border.
   b. Add *Blue, Accent 1, Lighter 80%* shading to the same sentence selected in Step 4a.
   c. Add a *Blue, Accent 1, 1½ point*, Shadow page border to the document.
   d. Insert an *Austin Quote* text box. Type the following text inside the box:
      Grand Canyon National Park is a World Heritage Site.
   e. Move the text box inserted at Step 4d so that the bottom of the text box aligns at the center of the page and bottom margin.
5. Save the revised document using the same name (**GrandCanyonPlanner-YourName**).
6. Leave the document open for Assessment 7.2; otherwise, close the document and submit the assessment to your instructor in the manner requested.

- Glossary
- Infographic
- Crossword Puzzle
- Multiple Choice
- Completion
- Matching
- Assessments
- Exercises
- Projects
- Skills Exam
- Chapter Exam

Assessment 7.2 Inserting, Formatting, and Modifying a Table into a Document

Type: Individual
Deliverable: National Park Trip Planner Document

Note: You must have completed Assessment 7.1 before starting this assessment.

1. If necessary, open **GrandCanyonPlanner-YourName**.
2. Position the insertion point at the end of the document text and press Enter until you create a new blank line at the left margin below the picture of Bright Angel Point.
3. Insert a 5 × 5 table and then type the following text in the table grid at the default table cell options:

Rim	Trail Name	Round Trip Distance	Round Trip Estimated Time	Elevation Change
South	Rim Trail	13 miles (21 km)	All day depending on desired distance	200 feet (60 m)
South	Bright Angel Trail	3 miles (4.8 km) to 9.2 miles (14.8 km)	From 2 to 9 hours depending on desired distance	2,112 feet (644 m) to 3,060 feet (933 m)
North	Bright Angel Point	0.5 miles (0.8 km)	30 minutes	200 feet (60 m)
North	Widforss Trail	10 miles (16 km)	6 hours	200 feet (60 m)

4. Format the table as follows:
   a. Apply a table style of your choosing.
   b. Deselect the *First Column* table style option if it is selected.
   c. Change the font size to 10 for all the text in the table cells.
5. Modify the layout of the table as follows:
   a. Set the width of the first column to 0.6 inches, and the third, fourth, and fifth columns to 1.5 inches.
   b. Align all table cells at the center horizontally and vertically.
   c. Insert a new row above row 4 and then type the following text in the new table cells:

South	Kaibab Trail	1.8 miles (2.9 km) to 6 miles (9.7 km)	From 1 to 6 hours depending on desired distance	600 feet (180 m) to 2,040 feet (622 m)

   d. Insert a new row at the bottom of the table and then type the following text in the table cells:

North	Kaibab Trail	1.4 miles (2.3 km) to 4 miles (6.4 km)	From 1 to 4 hours depending on desired distance	800 feet (245 m) to 1,450 feet (445 m)

6. If necessary, delete extra space above or below the table or decrease top and bottom margins to make sure the text box remains at the bottom center of the page.
7. Save the revised document using the same name (**GrandCanyonPlanner-YourName**).
8. Submit the assessment to your instructor in the manner requested.
9. Close the document.

Assessment 7.3 Completing a Research Report with Formatting, Citations, and Works Cited

Type: Individual
Deliverable: Academic Paper in MLA Format

1. Open **EtanerceptEssay**. If necessary, click the Enable Editing button to close Protected view.
2. Use Save As to change the file name to **EtanerceptEssay-YourName**, saving in the Ch7 folder within Assessments.
3. Select the entire document and change the font, line and paragraph spacing, and paragraph indents to conform to MLA guidelines (see Table 7.1 in Topic 7.6). *Hint: Turn on the display of nonprinting symbols to determine where paragraphs end to correctly complete the first line indent formatting.*
4. Insert your name, your instructor's name, the course title, and the current date at the top of the first page as per MLA guidelines (see Table 7.1, Topic 7.6).
5. Add page numbering one space after your last name at the right margin in a header. Format header text to same font and font size as rest of document.
6. Position the insertion point at the end of the quotation that reads "*The Etanercept injection is used . . . This medicine may also slow the progression of damage to the body from active arthritis or rheumatoid arthritis*", insert a space and then insert a citation referencing the following new source (leave fields blank where no information is provided):

Type of Source	Document From Web site
Author	Jarvis, B.; Faulds, D.
Name of Web Page	Etanercept: a review of its use in rheumatoid arthritis
Name of Web Site	PubMed, US National Library of Medicine
Year	1999
Month	June
Year Accessed	2021
Month Accessed	March
Day Accessed	15
Medium	Web

7. Position the insertion point at the end of the quotation that reads "*When Etanercept is administered alone . . . for at least 6 months*", insert a space and then cite the Jarvis and Faulds source.
8. Position the insertion point at the end of the indented quotation that reads "*Adverse effects of Etanercept are generally mild . . . cutaneous vasculitis, pancytopenia, and development of other autoimmune diseases*", insert a space and then insert a new citation referencing page 12 from the following new source:

Type of Source	Book
Author	(leave blank)
Title	Medication Guide: Enbrel (Etanercept)
Year	2011
City	Seattle
Publisher	Immunex Corporation
Medium	Print

9. Create and format a Works Cited page on a separate page at the end of the document.
10. Save the revised document using the same name (**EtanerceptEssay-YourName**).
11. Submit the assessment to your instructor in the manner requested and then close the document.

Assessment 7.4 Résumé and Cover Letter with Comments

Type: Individual
Deliverable: Personal Résumé and Cover Letter Targeted to a Specific Job Ad

1. Find a recent job ad for a position in your field of study.
2. Choose a résumé template that you like and create a new résumé for yourself that could be used as an application for the job ad.
3. Insert at least two comments in the résumé. Each comment should be associated with an entry in your résumé and pose a specific question to your instructor asking him or her for tips on how to improve the entry, or to provide additional explanation as to the writing style or tone that you used.
4. Choose a cover letter template that you like and write a cover letter to enclose with the résumé written specifically for the requirements in the job ad.
5. Add the URL or other source for the job ad that you used for this assessment in a comment associated with the current date text in the cover letter.
6. Save the résumé as **Resume-YourName** and save the cover letter as **CoverLetter-YourName**.
7. Submit the assessment to your instructor in the manner requested.

Assessment 7.5 Visual—Enhance and Format a Tourist Information Document

Type: Individual
Deliverable: Travel Information Flyer

1. Open **HangzhouInfo**. If necessary, click the Enable Editing button to close Protected view.
2. Format the document as shown in the Assessment 7.5 Hangzhou Informational Flyer on the next page, using the following formatting:
    a. The font is 11-point Book Antiqua for the body of the document and 16-point Book Antiqua for the title and subtitle.
    b. The subheadings have the Subtitle style applied and then formatted to 14-point Dark Blue font color.
    c. Substitute your name in the footer in place of *Student Name*.
    d. The image at the right margin is from the file **Hangzhou.jpg** with the Simple Frame, Black picture style; the image shown at the left margin is from the file **pagoda.png**; the text box is the *Grid Quote* with the font formatting changed to 12-point Book Antiqua and the case changed.
    e. Use your best judgment to match other formatting shown and not specified in Step 2.
3. Save the revised document as **HangzhouInfo-YourName** in the Ch7 folder within Assessments.
4. Submit the assessment to your instructor in the manner requested.
5. Close the document.

Assessment 7.5 Hangzhou Informational Flyer

Assessment 7.6 Audio—Composing a New Flyer

Type: Individual or Pairs
Deliverable: Food Drive Flyer

Create a flyer for the school's food drive campaign in support of the local food bank to be conducted on the fifteenth and sixteenth of next month. The organizer has left you a voice mail with details about the information to be included in the flyer.

1. Listen to the audio file **FoodDriveFlyer_instructions.** The file is located in the Ch7 folder in the StudentDataFiles folder on your storage medium.
2. Create the flyer including the details requested by the organizer in the voice mail.
3. Save the flyer in the Ch7 folder within the Assessments folder on your storage medium as **FoodDrive-YourName**.
4. Submit the assessment to your instructor in the manner requested.
5. Close the document.

Assessment 7.7 Go Mobile—Creating a Document for Rental Rates

Type: Individual
Deliverable: Word Document

1. Open the Word mobile app on your smartphone and start a new blank document.
2. Type today's date and then press Enter to move down to the next line.
3. Type Grand Canyon Bike Rentals and then press Enter to move down to the next line.

4. Type *Available March to January* and then press Enter.
5. Insert a table and type the following text in the table cells. If necessary, delete extra columns or rows added to the table when the table is created.

One hour	$12 plus tax
Half day	$30 plus tax
Full day	$40 plus tax

6. Use Save As to change the document name to **GCBikeRentals-YourName**, saving it in your OneDrive personal storage account.
7. Submit the assessment to your instructor in the manner requested.
8. Exit the Word mobile app.

Assessment 7.8 Job Ready—Composing a Visitor Information Flyer

Type: Individual, Pairs, or Teams
Deliverable: Document

You are helping to plan activities for a conference next year in Flagstaff, Arizona. A day before the official start of the conference has been left open to allow conference attendees time to explore the local area. You are tasked with creating a flyer with information about the Rim Trail day hike at the Grand Canyon. Assume those wanting to do the day hike will find their own transportation to the Grand Canyon National Park.

1. Research information about the Grand Canyon Rim Trail hike, including how to find it, length of the trail, condition of the trail, safety information, and so on.
2. Create a one-page flyer to be included with the conference kit that provides information about the hike that a registrant would need to know. Apply formatting and visual elements to make the flyer inviting and interesting to read.
3. Save the document as **RimTrailFlyer-YourName** in the Ch7 folder in the Assessments on your storage medium.
4. Submit the assessment to your instructor in the manner requested.

Assessment 7.9 Sending Assessment Work to OneNote Notebook

Type: Individual
Deliverable: New Page in Shared OneNote Notebook

1. Start OneNote and open the MyAssessments notebook created in Chapter 4, Assessment 4.4.
2. Make Word the active section and then add a new page titled *Chapter 7 Assessments*.
3. Switch to Word. For each assessment that you completed, open the document, use the *Export* option in the File backstage area to create a PDF of the document (using the default options), and then close the document. Switch back to OneNote. On the Chapter 7 Assessments page in the Word section in the MyAssessments notebook, insert each PDF printout in the order completed.
4. Close OneNote.
5. Close Word.
6. Submit the assessment to your instructor in the manner requested.

Creating, Editing, and Formatting Excel Worksheets

Chapter 8 Review and Assessment

The following assessments offer opportunities to apply what you have learned in relevant, real-world situations. Save your solution files and URLs, and submit them for evaluation as directed by your instructor.

Assessment 8.1 Creating and Editing a New Workbook

Type: Individual
Deliverable: Excel Worksheet with Auction Fee Calculations (Continued in Assessment 8.2)

1. Start a new blank workbook, change the width of column B to 12, and then enter text and values as shown below in Assessment 8.1 worksheet.
2. Save the workbook as **AuctionFees-YourName** in a new folder named *Ch8* within the Assessments folder on your storage medium.

	A	B	C	D	E	F	G	H	I	J
1	Video Game Online Auctions									
2	Fees for January Auctions									
3										
4	ID	Game Title			Platform	Sale Price	Fee	Shipping	Fee	Total Fee
5	25687	Shadow of the Tomb Raider			PS4 Pro	79.99		5.99		
6	31452	Marvel's Spider-Man			PS4 Pro	55.99		5.99		
7	98563	God of War			PS4 Pro	52.99		5.99		
8	17586	Red Dead Redemption 2			PS4 Pro	58.99		5.99		
9	32586	Call of Duty: Black Ops 4			Xbox One	56.99		5.99		
10	45862	Fallout 76			Xbox One	59.99		5.99		
11	13485	Assassin's Creed Odyssey			Xbox One	55.99		5.99		
12	65985	Forza Horizon 4			Xbox One	52.99		5.99		
13	74586	Fortnite Battle Royale			PC	9.99		0.75		
14	56842	PlayerUnknown's Battlegrounds			PC	22.99		2.3		
15	43668	Rise of the Tomb Raider			PC	49.99		4.75		

Assessment 8.1 Worksheet

3. Enter each of the following formulas using the typing or pointing method:
   G5 =F5*.10   J5   =G5+I5
   I5 =H5*.10
4. Use the fill handle to copy formulas to remaining rows in columns G, I, and J.
5. Type Total Fees Paid for January Auctions in B16.

6. Use the AutoSum button to calculate G16 and I16 totals. Flash Fill may automatically calculate the J16 total; if not, calculate the total yourself.
7. Edit the worksheet as follows:
   a. Change the sale price of Red Dead Redemption 2 from *58.99* to *61.79*.
   b. Edit the ID for Fallout 76 from *45862* to *86524*.
   c. Change the shipping for Rise of the Tomb Raider from *4.75* to *3.50*.
   d. Type the current year one space after *January* in A2 so that the entry reads *Fees for January 2021 Auctions*. (Your year will vary.)
   e. Type your name in A18.
8. Proofread carefully to make sure the worksheet is error-free.
9. Change the scaling option to fit all columns on one page.
10. Save the revised workbook using the same name (**AuctionFees-YourName**).
11. Leave the workbook open and continue to Assessment 8.2; otherwise, close the workbook and submit the assessment to your instructor in the manner requested.

Assessment 8.2 Editing and Formatting a Worksheet

Type: Individual
Deliverable: Excel Worksheet with Auction Fee Calculations

Note: You must have completed Assessment 8.1 before starting this assessment.

1. If necessary, open **AuctionFees-YourName**.
2. Use Save As to change the file name to **AuctionFeesFormatted-YourName**, saving it in the same folder.
3. Insert a new row above row 7, type the following auction item information in the appropriate cells, and insert formulas for the fees and total in columns G, I, and J:
   21549   Grand Theft Auto V   PS4 Pro 32.99 (sale price)   2.99 (shipping)
4. Insert a blank column between columns I and J so that the *Total Fee* column is set apart from the rest of the data.
5. Change the width of column B to *35* and then delete columns C and D.
6. Change the height of row 4 to *25* and middle-align the column headings.
7. Format the worksheet as follows:
   a. Merge and center the titles in row 1 and row 2 over columns A through I.
   b. Left-align A5:A16 and center-align E4 and G4.
   c. Apply Comma Style number format to D5:I17.
   d. Add a thick bottom border to A4:I4 and a top and bottom double border to E17, G17, and I17.
   e. Select A1:A2 and then change the font to Cambria, the font size to 16, the font color to Dark Blue, and apply bold formatting.
   f. Select A4:I4, apply bold formatting, and add Gold, Accent 4 shading.
   g. Apply bold formatting to B17, E17, G17, and I17.
8. Select A5:I16 and open the Sort dialog box. Sort the range by the *Game Title* column in ascending order. Deselect the range and review the new order of online auction data.
9. Change the worksheet to landscape orientation.
10. Save the revised workbook using the same name (**AuctionFeesFormatted-YourName**).
11. Turn on the display of cell formulas.

12. Display the worksheet in Print Preview and change the scaling option if necessary to fit the entire worksheet on one page. Exit the Print backstage area.
13. Use Save As to save a copy of the worksheet with the formulas displayed as **AuctionFeesFormulas-YourName**.
14. Submit the assessment to your instructor in the manner requested.
15. Close the workbook.

Assessment 8.3 Formatting with Styles and Inserting a New Worksheet

Type: Individual
Deliverable: Excel Workbook with Cancer Patient Statistics in Two Worksheets

1. Open **CancerStatsReport**. Click the Enable Editing button, if necessary, to close Protected view.
2. Use Save As to change the file name to **CancerStatsReport-YourName**, saving it in the Ch8 folder in Assessments.
3. Merge and center the titles in row 1 and row 2 over columns A through G.
4. Wrap the text in A3:G3.
5. Change the column widths as follows:
    Column B to *10*   Column C to *9*   Column E to *10*   Column F to *20*
6. Apply cell styles of your choosing to A1, A2, and A3:G3 to improve the appearance of the worksheet.
7. Insert a new worksheet in the workbook and change the name to *Quarter 2*.
8. Rename the ReportData worksheet *Quarter 1*.
9. Copy A1:G3 from the Quarter 1 sheet and paste it to A1 in the Quarter 2 sheet, keeping the source column widths. Edit the title in A2 so that the title references Quarter 2 instead of Quarter 1.
10. Copy A4:G30 from the Quarter 1 sheet and paste it to A4 in the Quarter 2 sheet.
11. In the Quarter 2 sheet, clear the contents of A4:A30 and G4:G30.
12. Set the print settings for each worksheet to *Fit All Columns on One Page*.
13. Freeze the first three rows in each worksheet.
14. Save the revised workbook using the same name (**CancerStatsReport-YourName**).
15. Submit the assessment to your instructor in the manner requested.
16. Close the workbook.

Assessment 8.4 Creating a Weekly Schedule from a Template

Type: Individual
Deliverable: Worksheet with a Schedule for the Current Week

1. You learned about creating new documents from templates in Word in Chapter 6. Excel also has many templates available for creating new workbooks that are grouped into categories and located using the search text box in the New backstage area. Search for and select a template of your choosing to create a weekly schedule. Use the search phrase *time schedule* to find a suitable template.
2. Enter your schedule for the current week into the new worksheet. Make sure the schedule is complete with all of your classes and other activities.
3. Save the workbook in the Ch8 folder within Assessments as **WeeklySchedule-YourName**.
4. Submit the assessment to your instructor in the manner requested.
5. Close the workbook.

Assessment 8.5 Visual—Creating a Party Expense Worksheet

Type: Individual
Deliverable: Anniversary Party Expense Worksheet

1. Create a worksheet similar to the Assessment 8.5 worksheet below, with the following information:
   a. The amounts in the *Difference* column are formulas that calculate the actual expenses minus the estimated expenses, and the values shown in row 12 are formulas.
   b. The width of column A is 42, and the width of columns B, C, and D is 12. The height of row 1 is 36 and the height of row 2 is 24.
   c. A2:D2 has the Accent6 cell style applied.
   d. The font used in A1 is 18-point Cambria. The font for the rest of the cells in the worksheet is Book Antiqua at the default size.
   e. Use your best judgment for any other format options such as alignment and shading.
2. Save the worksheet in the Ch8 folder within the Assessments folder as **PartyExpenses-YourName**.
3. Submit the assessment to your instructor in the manner requested.
4. Close the workbook.

	A	B	C	D
1	Mom and Dad's Anniversary Party Budget			
2	Item	Estimated	Actual	Difference
3	Decorations	$ 325.00	$ 342.00	$ 17.00
4	Flowers	625.00	601.00 -	24.00
5	Entertainer	550.00	550.00	-
6	Photographer and prints	875.00	1,125.00	250.00
7	Rental of reception room	150.00	150.00	-
8	Rental of tables, chairs, plates, and cutlery	190.00	175.00 -	15.00
9	Food and drinks	2,245.00	2,100.00 -	145.00
10	Invitations	75.00	81.00	6.00
11	Miscellaneous supplies	100.00	112.00	12.00
12	Total Expenses	$ 5,135.00	$ 5,236.00	$ 101.00

Assessment 8.5 Worksheet

Assessment 8.6 Audio—Internet Research and Composing a New Workbook

Type: Individual or Pairs
Deliverable: Excel Workbook with Costs for a Spring Break Trip

You are asked to help the president of the student union at your school create a workbook with costs for five popular spring break destinations for a prize that includes a free trip with spending money. The student union office assistant has left you a phone message explaining what to include in the workbook.

1. Listen to the audio file **SpringBreakContest_instructions**.
2. Complete the research and compose the worksheet as instructed.
3. Save the workbook in the Ch8 folder within Assessments as **SpringBreakContest-YourName**.
4. Submit the assessment to your instructor in the manner requested.
5. Close the workbook.

Review & Assessment Chapter 8 Creating, Editing, and Formatting Excel Worksheets RA-39

Assessment 8.7 Go Mobile—Creating a Catering Estimate Worksheet

Type: Individual
Deliverable: Excel Workbook with Catering Estimate

1. If necessary, download and install the Microsoft Excel Mobile app to your smartphone. Open the Excel Mobile app and start a new blank workbook.
2. Type today's date and then press Enter to move down to the next cell.
3. Type Catering Estimate and then press Enter to move down to the next cell.
4. Type SkyValue Catering and then press Enter.
5. Enter the data in the cells indicated below.

	A	B	C
4		Per Person	
5	Breakfast	6.99	
6	Lunch	12.99	
7	Dinner	18.99	
8			
9	Estimated guests:		110
10			
11	Catering Cost:		

6. Create a formula in C11 that calculates the total catering estimate using the following example and substituting cell references where needed: =(estimated guests*breakfast cost)+(estimated guests*lunch cost)+(estimated guests*dinner cost).
7. Type your name in A13.
8. Use Save As to change the workbook name to **CateringEstimate-YourName**, saving it in your OneDrive personal storage account.
9. Submit the assessment to your instructor in the manner requested.
10. Exit the Excel Mobile app.

Assessment 8.8 Job Ready—Composing a Salary Analysis Worksheet

Type: Individual, Pairs, or Teams
Deliverable: Worksheet with Average Salaries

Job interview applicants are often asked to provide their expected starting salary if hired by the company. Being prepared to answer this question with a reasonable salary range will give you confidence in the next job interview.

1. Research salaries for an entry-level position in your field of study. Find at least five resources with starting salary ranges.
2. Create a worksheet that summarizes the five salary ranges you found. At the bottom of the data, create a formula that calculates the average from the five salaries. Add an appropriate label to describe the calculated value.
3. Format the worksheet by applying cell styles to improve the appearance of the data. Adjust column widths as necessary and make any other formatting changes you think are needed.
4. Add a new worksheet and rename it *URLs*. In the URLs worksheet, enter the website addresses for the salary information you used.
5. Rename the Sheet1 worksheet *Salary Info*.
6. Save the workbook as **SalaryResearch-YourName** in the Ch8 folder in Assessments.
7. Submit the assessment to your instructor in the manner requested.

Assessment 8.9 Sending Assessment Work to OneNote Notebook

Type: Individual
Deliverable: New Page in OneNote Notebook

1. Start OneNote and open the MyAssessments notebook you created in Chapter 4, Assessment 4.4.
2. Make Excel the active section and then type Chapter 8 Assessments as the page title.
3. Switch to Excel. For each Chapter 8 assessment that you completed, open the file, use the *Export* option on the File tab to create a PDF of the worksheet (using the default options), and then close the workbook. Switch back to OneNote. On the Chapter 8 Assessments page in the Excel section in the MyAssessments notebook, insert each PDF printout in order completed. Make sure to include all worksheets in workbooks with more than one sheet tab.
4. Close OneNote.
5. Close Excel.
6. Submit the assessment to your instructor in the manner requested.

Inserting Functions and Enhancing an Excel Worksheet

Chapter 9

Review and Assessment

The following assessments offer opportunities to apply what you have learned in relevant, real-world situations. Save your solution files and URLs, and submit them for evaluation as directed by your instructor.

Assessment 9.1 Adding Statistical, Date, Financial, and Logical Functions to a Workbook

Type: Individual
Deliverable: Worksheet with Auction Fee Financial Analysis and Mortgage Options

1. Open **AuctionFeesandMortgagePlanner**. If necessary, click the Enable Editing button to close Protected view.
2. Use Save As to change the file name to **AuctionFeesandMortgagePlanner-YourName** in a new folder named *Ch9* within the Assessments folder on your storage medium.
3. In J2 enter a formula that will insert the current date and update the date each time the workbook is opened or printed.
4. Assign the following names to the cells indicated:
   C2   AuctionFee   G2   PaymentFee
5. Complete the formulas required in the worksheet using the following information:
   a. In column B, calculate the payment due dates as 5 days following the auction end date.
   b. In column D, calculate the auction fees as the sale price times the auction fee percentage. Use the range name created in Step 4 in the formula.
   c. In column E, calculate the payment processing fees as the sale price times the payment processing percentage. Use the range name created in Step 4 in the formula.
   d. In column F, calculate the net auction earnings as the sale price minus the auction fee and payment processing fee.
   e. In column G, calculate the amount to transfer to the checking account as the value that resides in net auction earnings for those instances in which the net auction earnings are less than or equal to $20.00; otherwise, calculate the amount as 50 percent of the net auction earnings.
   f. In column H, calculate the amount to transfer to the investment account as 50 percent of the net auction earnings for those instances in which the net auction earnings are more than $20.00; otherwise, show zero in the cell.

- Glossary
- Infographic
- Crossword Puzzle
- Multiple Choice
- Completion
- Matching
- Assessments
- Exercises
- Projects
- Skills Exam
- Chapter Exam

g. In column J, calculate the three sets of required statistics. Use the labels to help you determine the functions and arguments required.
h. In row 27, calculate totals for columns C through H.
6. Format C2 and G2 to Percent Style, format the dates in columns A and B to the style *14-Mar*, and format all other values to Comma Style.
7. Make MortgageAnalysis the active worksheet and complete the formulas required in the worksheet using the following information:
   a. In B7 and D7, calculate the estimated monthly payments.
   b. In B9 and D9, calculate the total paid over the life of each mortgage.
8. For each worksheet, change page layout options as necessary to make sure the worksheet will fit on one page centered horizontally and with your name centered in a header, the file name at the left margin in a footer, and the sheet name at the right margin in a footer.
9. Save the revised workbook using the same name (**AuctionFeesandMortgagePlanner-YourName**).
10. Close the workbook.
11. Submit the assessment to your instructor in the manner requested.

Assessment 9.2 Creating and Modifying Charts

Type: Individual
Deliverable: Worksheet with Charts Illustrating Vacation Destination Statistics

1. Open **VacDestinations**. If necessary, click the Enable Editing button to close Protected view.
2. Use Save As to change the file name to **VacDestinations-YourName**, saving in the Ch9 folder within Assessments.
3. With the TopVacDestinations sheet active, create a pie chart at the bottom left of the worksheet area that graphs the Worldwide destinations and percentages. Create a second pie chart at the bottom right of the worksheet area that graphs the United States and Canada destinations and percentages. Add and/or modify chart elements you think are appropriate to make sure the charts are easy to read and understand.
4. With the NationalParks worksheet active, create a clustered column chart that graphs the national parks and visitors. Position the chart where you think the chart looks good, and add and/or modify chart elements you think are appropriate to make sure the chart is easy to read and understand.
5. With the InternationalTravel worksheet active, select A3:D15 and create a line chart in a chart sheet named *InternationalTravelChart*. Add and/or modify chart elements you think are appropriate to make sure the chart is easy to read and understand.
6. For all worksheets, change page layout options as necessary to make sure the worksheet will fit on one page centered horizontally and with your name centered in a header, the file name at the left margin in a footer, and the sheet name at the right margin in a footer. **Hint:** *Add the header and footer in the InternationalTravelChart sheet using the Page Setup hyperlink in Print Preview.*
7. Save the revised workbook using the same name (**VacDestinations-YourName**).
8. Close the workbook.
9. Submit the assessment to your instructor in the manner requested.

Review & Assessment Chapter 9 Inserting Functions and Enhancing an Excel Worksheet   **RA-43**

Assessment 9.3 Adding Sparklines and Comments

Type: Individual
Deliverable: Worksheet with Comments and Sparklines Illustrating School Newspaper Budget Values

1. Open **SchoolPaperBudget**. If necessary, click the Enable Editing button to close Protected view.
2. Use Save As to change the file name to **SchoolPaperBudget-YourName**, saving in the Ch9 folder within Assessments.
3. Create line sparkline charts in column K that graph the budget values for September through April. Show the high and low points. Add or modify any other sparkline elements you think are appropriate.
4. Add the following comments to the cells indicated:
   E9   Christmas ads expected to increase 10% this year.
   I5   New ISP contract takes effect in April.
   I9   Consider end-of-year special pricing to raise ad revenue.
5. Set the print option that prints comments on a separate page after the worksheet.
6. Save the revised workbook using the same name (**SchoolPaperBudget-YourName**).
7. Close the workbook.
8. Submit the assessment to your instructor in the manner requested.

Assessment 9.4 Working with Tables

Type: Individual
Deliverable: Worksheet with Model Home Pricing Table

1. Open **ModelHomes**. If necessary, click the Enable Editing button to close Protected view.
2. Use Save As to change the file name to **ModelHomes-YourName**, saving in the Ch9 folder within Assessments.
3. Format A5:E20 as a table.
4. Change to a table style of your choosing.
5. Sort in ascending order by the *Description of upgrade* column.
6. Add totals below each model home that sum the total cost of the upgrades.
7. In A23 enter the text TOTAL MODEL HOME PRICE WITH ALL UPGRADES.
8. Create formulas in B23:E23 that show the total price of each model home with the base price and total upgrade costs.
9. Change the worksheet to landscape orientation, centered vertically, and with your name centered in a header and the file name centered in a footer.
10. Save the revised workbook using the same name (**ModelHomes-YourName**).
11. Close the workbook.
12. Submit the assessment to your instructor in the manner requested.

Assessment 9.5 Visual—Creating a Worksheet and Charts to Show Food Drive Results

Type: Individual
Deliverable: Worksheet with Food Drive Results and Charts

1. Create a worksheet and charts similar to the one shown in the Assessment 9.5 worksheet on the next page with the following additional information:
   a. The workbook theme is *Frame*.
   b. The charts are clustered bar charts using *Style 13*.

c. Set the height for row 1 to *30.00* and row 2 to *21.00*. Set the width of column A to *16.50* and column B to *10.00*.
d. The font size for row 1 is 18 points and row 2 is 12 points.
e. Use your best judgment for any other format options such as shading.
2. Save the worksheet in the Ch9 folder within Assessments as **FoodDrive-YourName**.
3. Change the top margin to 1.5 inches. Make sure the worksheet will fit on one page in portrait orientation with your name centered in a header and the file name centered in a footer.
4. Save the workbook again using the same name (**FoodDrive-YourName**).
5. Close the workbook.
6. Submit the assessment to your instructor in the manner requested.

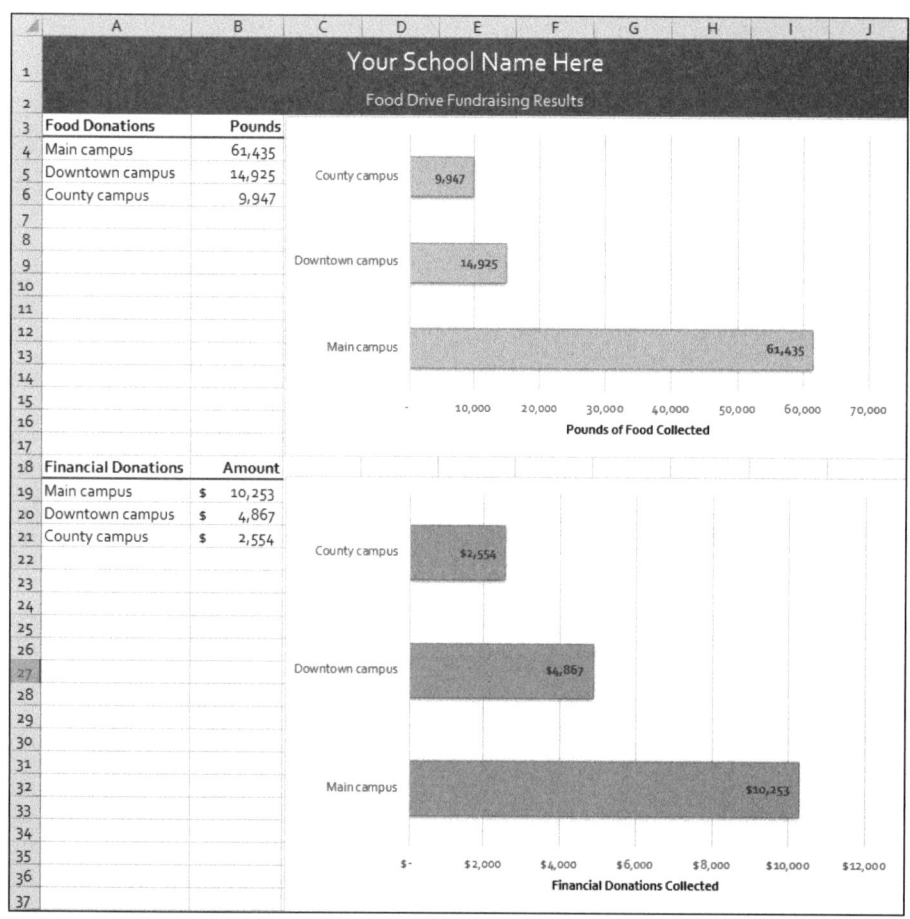

Assessment 9.5 Food Drive Worksheet and Charts

Assessment 9.6 Audio—Internet Research and Composing a New Workbook

Type: Individual or Pairs
Deliverable: Worksheet with Membership Statistical Data and Line Chart

The academic manager of the business school has asked for your help preparing a worksheet and line chart with membership statistics from the launch of the Instagram social media website in October 2010 to today. The school assistant has left you a voice mail with instructions.

1. Listen to the audio file **InstagramUserData_instructions**.
2. Complete the research and compose the worksheet and chart as instructed.

3. Save the workbook in the Ch9 folder within Assessments as **InstagramUserData-YourName**.
4. Close the workbook.
5. Submit the assessment to your instructor in the manner requested.

Assessment 9.7 Go Mobile—Calculating a Student Loan Payment

Type: Individual
Deliverable: Excel Workbook with Student Loan Payment

1. Open the Excel Mobile app and start a new blank workbook.
2. Type Student Loan Planner and then press Enter twice to move down to cell A3.
3. Enter the data in the cells indicated below. Allow the text in column A to overflow into column B.

	A	B	C
3	Loan amount		25000
4	Annual interest rate		5.05%
5	Term		10
6			
7	Monthly payment		

4. Create a PMT formula in C7 that calculates the estimated monthly payment for the loan. *Note: The result will appear as a negative value because the loan amount is typed as a positive amount in C3. Since the loan payment is an amount that you have to pay out, showing the payment as a negative value is preferred by some people.*
5. Type your name in A9.
6. Apply formatting options of your choosing to improve the appearance of the worksheet.
7. Use Save As to change the workbook name to **StudentLoanPlanner -YourName**, saving it in your OneDrive personal storage account.
8. Submit the workbook to your instructor in the manner requested.
9. Exit the Excel Mobile app.

Assessment 9.8 Job Ready—Planning a Budget for Entry-Level Salary

Type: Individual, Pairs, or Teams
Deliverable: Workbook with Budget for an Entry-Level Graduate

An important part of a job search after graduation is knowing in advance the cost of living in the geographic area you plan to work. In Assessment 8.8, you researched the average salary for an entry-level position in your field of study. In this assessment, you will continue job search preparation by determining whether the average salary provides enough money to live comfortably where you want to work.

1. Research the cost of living in the city you plan to work after graduation. Make sure you include all the standard costs one would incur living independently, such as housing, transportation, food, internet, cell phone, clothing, supplies, and entertainment.
2. Create a worksheet with the estimated costs and calculate the total. You decide the best way to organize the costs and whether you want to present the information monthly or annually.

3. Add the salary that you expect to earn to the worksheet. Use the average salary you calculated in the worksheet completed in Assessment 8.8. Make sure to include a cost item for government payroll taxes, or enter the salary at the net pay you expect to receive. If necessary, search for an online net pay calculator tool that will give you an estimate of your take-home pay.
4. Include a formula that calculates the amount left over after paying all the living costs from the expected take-home pay.
5. Apply formatting options of your choosing to improve the appearance of the worksheet.
6. Add a new worksheet and rename it *URLs*. In the URLs worksheet, enter the website addresses for the information you used.
7. Rename the Sheet1 worksheet *MyBudget*.
8. Save the workbook as **MyBudget-YourName** in the Ch9 folder in Assessments.
9. Submit the assessment to your instructor in the manner requested.

Assessment 9.9 OneNote—Sending Assessment Work to OneNote Notebook

Type: Individual
Deliverable: New Page in Shared OneNote Notebook

1. Start OneNote and open the MyAssessments notebook created in Chapter 4, Assessment 4.4.
2. Make Excel the active section and add a new page titled *Chapter 9 Assessments*.
3. Switch to Excel. For each assessment that you completed, open the workbook, use the Export option on the File tab to create a PDF of the worksheet (using the default options), and then close the workbook. Switch back to OneNote. On the Chapter 9 Assessments page in the Excel section in the MyAssessments notebook, insert each PDF printout in order completed. Make sure to include all worksheets in workbooks with more than one sheet tab.
4. Close OneNote.
5. Close Excel.
6. Submit the assessment to your instructor in the manner requested.

Creating, Editing, and Formatting a PowerPoint Presentation

Chapter 10 Review and Assessment

The following assessments offer opportunities to apply what you have learned in relevant, real-world situations. Save your solution files and URLs, and submit them for evaluation as directed by your instructor.

Assessment 10.1 Creating and Editing a New Presentation

Type: Individual
Deliverable: Presentation about World and US Landmarks (Continued in Assessments 10.2 and 10.3)

1. Start a new presentation, choosing a theme and variant that you like.
2. Save the presentation as **Landmarks-YourName** in a new folder named *Ch10* within the Assessments folder on your storage medium.
3. Create slides including multilevel lists, a table, and a comparison slide with the following information:

Slide 1	Title	Famous Landmarks
	Subtitle	Your Name
Slide 2	Title	World and National Landmarks
	List	Top 5 World Landmarks
		Top 5 US Landmarks
		Survey Results
		Honorable Mentions
Slide 3	Title	Top 5 World Landmarks
	Multilevel List	The Pyramid of Khufu
		Located in Giza, Egypt
		Largest pyramid ever built
		The Great Wall of China
		Completed during the Ming dynasty (1368 to 1644)
		Acropolis
		UNESCO World Heritage Site
		Parthenon Greek temple
		Eiffel Tower
		18,000 metallic parts joined by 2,500,000 rivets
		Taj Mahal
		Agra, India

- Glossary
- Infographic
- Crossword Puzzle
- Multiple Choice
- Completion
- Matching
- Assessments
- Exercises
- Projects
- Skills Exam
- Chapter Exam

Slide 4	Title	Top 5 US Landmarks	
	List	Statue of Liberty, New York	
		Grand Canyon, Arizona	
		Mount Rushmore, South Dakota	
		Independence Hall, Pennsylvania	
		The National Mall, District of Columbia	
Slide 5	Title	Survey Results	
	Table	Social Media Website	Votes Cast
		Facebook	345,985
		Instagram	295,672
		Twitter	420,870
		Tumblr	155,329
Slide 6	Title	Honorable Mentions	
	Comparison	World Landmarks	US Landmarks
	Slide Layout	Stonehenge, UK	Freedom Trail, Boston
		Edinburgh Castle, Scotland	Fort Sumter, Charleston
		Buckingham Palace, UK	The Alamo, San Antonio
		Machu Picchu, Peru	Gateway Arch, St. Louis

4. Perform a spell check and carefully proofread each slide, making corrections as needed.
5. Edit Slide 3 as follows:
    a. Delete the entry *Largest pyramid ever built.*
    b. Delete the entry *UNESCO World Heritage Site.*
    c. Insert the text *Tower located in Paris has* before the entry that begins *18,000 metallic parts.*
    d. Insert the text *Marble mausoleum located in* before *Agra, India.*
6. Edit Slide 5, changing the votes cast by Facebook from *345,985* to *543,589.*
7. Save the revised presentation using the same name (**Landmarks-YourName**).
8. Leave the presentation open if you are continuing to Assessment 10.2; otherwise close the presentation and submit the assessment to your instructor in the manner requested.

Assessment 10.2 Editing and Formatting a Presentation

Type: Individual
Deliverable: Presentation about World and US Landmarks (Continued in Assessment 10.3)

Note: You must have completed Assessment 10.1 before starting this assessment.

1. If necessary, open **Landmarks-YourName**.
2. Change the theme and variant to another design of your choosing. Check each slide after you change the theme for corrections that may be needed. For example, a theme that uses the All Caps font in a title or subtitle may cause changes in capitalization when the theme is changed to one that does not use the All Caps font.

3. Display the slide master and make the following changes to the top slide in the hierarchy:
   a. Change the font color for all the titles to another font color of your choosing.
   b. Change the bullet character to a different symbol and color than the one used in the theme.
4. Display Slide 5 and modify the table layout and design as follows:
   a. Change the width of the first column to 3.5 inches.
   b. Change the width of the second column to 1.75 inches.
   c. Center-align the entries in the second column.
   d. Change the table style to another style of your choosing.
   e. Move the table so that the table is approximately centered horizontally and vertically on the slide. **Hint:** *Use the smart guides to help you with the placement.*
5. Display Slide 6 and make the following changes:
   a. Change the bullet character to a different symbol than the symbol that was used on the slide master for each of the two lists.
   b. Resize the left list placeholder so that the right border ends just after the longest entry in the list without the text wrapping to a second line. Resize the left title placeholder to the same width as the list.
   c. Move the left title and list placeholders closer to the right title and list. Align the two titles and lists so that they are approximately centered horizontally on the slide.
6. Save the revised presentation using the same name (**Landmarks-YourName**).
7. Leave the presentation open if you are continuing to Assessment 10.3; otherwise, close the presentation and submit the assessment to your instructor in the manner requested.

Assessment 10.3 Rearranging Slides and Adding Notes and Comments

Type: Individual
Deliverable: Presentation about World and US Landmarks

Note: *You must have completed Assessments 10.1 and 10.2 before starting this assessment.*
1. If necessary, open **Landmarks-YourName**.
2. Move the *Survey Results* slide so that it becomes the third slide in the slide deck.
3. Move the *Honorable Mentions* slide after the *Survey Results* slide.
4. Display Slide 2 and edit the bulleted list to reposition the bottom two bulleted list items so they become the top two bulleted list items.
5. Display the *Survey Results* slide and then type the following text in the notes pane: Our first survey using social media for reader voting was a phenomenal success. Plans for next year's survey are to expand voting to include other social media sites. Ask the audience for suggestions.
6. Display the *Honorable Mentions* slide and then type the following text in the notes pane: All honorable mentions had at least 20,000 votes.
7. Display the *Top 5 World Landmarks* slide, select the bulleted list text below *Eiffel Tower*, and then type the following comment: Should I remove the number of parts and rivets?
8. Display the *Top 5 US Landmarks* slide and then type the following comment for the entire slide: Should I add the number of votes for each landmark?
9. Save the revised presentation using the same name (**Landmarks-YourName**).
10. Submit the assessment to your instructor in the manner requested and then close the presentation.

Assessment 10.4 Internet Research and Creating a Presentation from a Template

Type: Individual or Pairs
Deliverable: Presentation about Inventions

1. Start a new presentation, browsing the *Education* category of templates and choosing a template that you like.
2. Create slides for a presentation about the inventions listed below. For each invention, research four to five interesting facts about the invention and add the information in a bulleted list on the slide.
   - Slide 1 (You determine an appropriate title and subtitle.)
   - Slide 2 (You determine an appropriate introductory slide for the presentation.)
   - Slide 3 The Telephone
   - Slide 4 The Television
   - Slide 5 The Automobile
   - Slide 6 The Lightbulb
3. Delete slides that were downloaded as part of the template that are not needed for this presentation.
4. Save the presentation in the Ch10 folder within the Assessments folder as **Inventions-YourName**.
5. Submit the assessment to your instructor in the manner requested.
6. Close the presentation.

Assessment 10.5 Visual—Creating a Graduation Party Planning Presentation

Type: Individual
Deliverable: Presentation on College Graduation Party Planning

1. Create a presentation similar to the one shown in the Assessment 10.5 Graduation Party Planning Presentation on the next page with the following additional information:
   a. The theme is Integral with one of the variants selected.
   b. The bullet symbols have been changed on the slide master.
   c. The font color for the slide titles has been changed on the slide master. Use your best judgment to choose a similar color.
   d. Use your best judgment to determine other formatting, placeholder size, and alignment options.
2. Save the presentation in the Ch10 folder within the Assessments folder as **GradParty-YourName**.
3. Submit the assessment to your instructor in the manner requested.
4. Close the presentation.

GRADUATION PARTY PLANNING
Student name

GRADUATION PARTY CHECKLIST
Date and venue
Budget
Invitations
Plan food, decorations, and entertainment

CHOOSE THE DATE AND VENUE
Survey close friends and family before setting the date
☐ Find a date that conflicts the least with other events

Visit possible venues
☐ Indoors
  ○ Restaurants, banquet or community halls
☐ Outdoors
  ○ Local park, recreation area, or estate

BUDGET

Expense	Typical Budget
Location, Food, and Drinks	$500 to $750
Invitations	$100 to $150
Decorations	$100 to $150
Incidental Expenses	$100

INVITATIONS
Finalize the guest list
Send out invitations four to six weeks in advance
Set the RSVP date three weeks before party

FOOD, DECORATIONS & ENTERTAINMENT
Choose caterer
☐ Ask for recommendations from friends or family

Decorate around a theme
☐ Choose a theme related to your program

Entertainment
☐ Assemble your favorite music playlists
☐ Plan to tell a few humorous stories from school

Assessment 10.5 Graduation Party Planning Presentation

Audio ▸ **Assessment 10.6 Audio—Internet Research and Composing a New Presentation**

Type: Individual or Pairs
Deliverable: Presentation about US or Canadian Historical Figure

You have been asked to help the president of the school history society with a presentation for a guest speaker for a new activity called "History Conversations." You've received a voice mail that tells you about the premiere History Conversations event next month.

1. Listen to the audio file **HistoricalFigure_Instructions**.
2. Complete the research about a US or Canadian historical figure and his or her significance in history and compose the presentation as instructed.
3. Save the presentation in the Ch10 folder within the Assessments folder as **HistoricalFigure-YourName**.
4. Submit the assessment to your instructor in the manner requested.
5. Close the presentation.

Mobile ▸ **Assessment 10.7 Go Mobile—Creating a New Presentation**

Type: Individual
Deliverable: Presentation about Company Culture

1. If necessary, download and install the Microsoft PowerPoint mobile app to your smartphone. Open the PowerPoint mobile app, start a new blank presentation, and then choose a template that you like.
2. Create slides for a presentation on corporate culture as follows:

Slide 1	Title	Company Culture
	Subtitle	Your Name
Slide 2	Title	What is Company Culture?
	List	Values, beliefs, and attitudes that drive employee actions
		Defines the work environment for employees
		Partly expressed in mission and values statements
Slide 3	Title	Why is Culture Important?
	List	Employees happier when they fit well with culture
		Employees more productive when they understand culture
		Able to attract top talent
		Less employee turnover

3. Perform a spell check and carefully proofread each slide.
4. Use Save As to change the presentation name to **CompanyCulture-YourName**, saving it in your OneDrive personal storage account.
5. Submit the presentation to your instructor in the manner requested.
6. Exit the PowerPoint mobile app.

Assessment 10.8 Job Ready—Internet Research and Composing a New Presentation

Type: Individual, Pairs, or Teams
Deliverable: Presentation about Assessing a Company Culture

Finding a job at a company with a culture that suits your work preferences is important. For example, one company may have a formal management structure in place with many written rules and regulations. Another workplace may have few managers, a casual atmosphere, and few written rules. Company culture may be implied and not expressly defined.

1. Research methods to learn about a company culture when job hunting.
2. Create a presentation with an appropriate title slide followed by six slides minimum to eight slides maximum that summarize your research in bulleted list points.
3. Add a slide at the end with the URLs that you used to complete this assessment.
4. Save the presentation as **AssessCulture-YourName** in the Ch10 folder in the Assessments folder on your USB flash drive.
5. Submit the assessment to your instructor in the manner requested.

Assessment 10.9 Sending Assessment Work to OneNote Notebook

Type: Individual
Deliverable: New Page in Shared OneNote Notebook

1. Start OneNote and open the MyAssessments notebook created in Chapter 4, Assessment 4.4.
2. Make PowerPoint the active section and then type Chapter 10 Assessments as the page title.
3. Switch to PowerPoint. Open the presentation for each assessment you completed. Use the Export option on the File tab to create a PDF of the presentation (using the default options), and then close the presentation. Switch to OneNote. On the Chapter 10 Assessments page in the PowerPoint section in the My Assessments notebook, insert each PDF printout in order completed.
4. Close OneNote.
5. Close PowerPoint.
6. Submit the assessment to your instructor in the manner requested.

Enhancing a Presentation with Multimedia and Animation Effects

Chapter 11 Review and Assessment

The following assessments offer opportunities to apply what you have learned in relevant, real-world situations. Save your solution files and URLs, and submit them for evaluation as directed by your instructor.

Assessment 11.1 Adding Graphics to a Presentation

Type: Individual
Deliverable: Presentation about World War I (Continued in Assessments 11.2 and 11.3)

1. Open **WorldWarIPres**. If necessary, click the Enable Editing button to close Protected view.
2. Use Save As to change the file name to **WorldWarIPres-YourName** in a new folder named *Ch11* within the Assessments folder on your storage medium.
3. Make Slide 2 the active slide in the slide pane and then insert the image **MilitaryGroupWWI.jpg** at the bottom right of the slide, resizing the image as needed.
4. Make Slide 6 the active slide in the slide pane and then insert the picture **WeaponWWI.jpg** at the right side of the slide next to the bulleted list, resizing the image as needed.
5. Make Slide 3 the active slide in the slide pane and then convert the bulleted list to a SmartArt graphic. You determine an appropriate SmartArt layout. Apply a SmartArt Style of your choosing. Resize and make other formatting changes you think are appropriate.
6. Make Slide 4 the active slide in the slide pane and then convert the bulleted list to the same SmartArt layout you used on Slide 3. Apply the same design and formatting changes so that Slide 3 and Slide 4 are consistent.
7. Make Slide 5 the active slide in the slide pane and then insert a chart using the following information:
    a. Choose the *Bar* category and the *Clustered Bar* chart type.
    b. Enter the following data in the worksheet. Delete columns and rows with sample data that are not needed for the chart.
        A2: Allied Forces   B2 12.6
        A3: Central Forces   B3 8.4

- Glossary
- Infographic
- Crossword Puzzle
- Multiple Choice
- Completion
- Matching
- Assessments
- Exercises
- Projects
- Skills Exam
- Chapter Exam

c. Delete the *Series 1* legend that appears below the chart.
d. Edit the *Series 1* chart title that appears above the chart to read Millions of Soldiers.
e. Apply a chart style of your choosing.
8. Insert a shape positioned near the top right of the chart on Slide 5 using the *Explosion 8 Points* option in the *Stars and Banners* category with the following text inside: *Allies bear 4.2 million more injuries!* Resize the shape to accommodate the text, allowing the shape to flow outside the chart border. Apply a shape style of your choosing.
9. Insert a text box positioned below the picture on Slide 6 with the following text inside the box: *Canadian artillery loading a field gun.* Change the font size to 14 points and italicize the text.
10. Insert a text box positioned below the chart on Slide 5 and aligned at the left edge with the following text inside the box: *Source: Military Research, UK.* Italicize the text.
11. Insert a new slide after Slide 7 with a Title Only layout and type the following text as the slide title: 100 Year Anniversary. Create a WordArt object of your choice with the text: 2014 to 2018. Change the font size to 72 points and format the text with WordArt styles and text effects of your choosing.
12. Save the revised presentation using the same name (**WorldWarIPres-YourName**).
13. Leave the presentation open if you are continuing to Assessment 11.2; otherwise, close the presentation and submit the assessment to your instructor in the manner requested.

Assessment 11.2 Adding Sound and Video

Type: Individual
Deliverable: Presentation about World War I (Continued in Assessment 11.3)

Note: You must have completed Assessment 11.1 before starting this assessment.
1. If necessary, open **WorldWarIPres-YourName**.
2. Make Slide 7 with the title *American Forces in France* the active slide in the slide pane.
3. Insert the video clip **AmericaGoesToWar.wmv** from the Ch11 folder in StudentDataFiles on the slide. Edit the video as follows:
   a. Change the *Start* option to *Automatically*.
   b. Trim the video to start at *0:48* and end at *2:35*.
   c. Apply a video style of your choosing to the video object.
4. Add the audio clip **BulletsandBayonets.mp3** from the Ch11 folder in StudentDataFiles on Slide 1 with the following audio options:
   a. Change the *Start* option to *Automatically*.
   b. Change the volume to *Low*.
   c. Set the audio to play across all slides.
   d. Hide the sound icon during a slide show.
5. Type the following photo, video, and audio credits in a table on the last slide. You determine the table style, column widths, and other format options.

Slide	Item	Credit
1	Music	United States Marine Band at George Mason University
2	Photo	City of Toronto archives via Wikimedia Commons
6	Photo	Canadian Department of National Defence via Wikimedia Commons
7	Video	America Goes Over (Part I), US Army, Signal Corps via Internet Archive

6. Save the revised presentation using the same name (**WorldWarIPres-YourName**).
7. Leave the presentation open if you are continuing to Assessment 11.3; otherwise, close the presentation and submit the assessment to your instructor in the manner requested.

Assessment 11.3 Adding Transition and Animation Effects and Setting Up a Slide Show

Type: Individual
Deliverable: Self-Running Presentation about World War I

Note: You must have completed Assessments 11.1 and 11.2 before starting this assessment.

1. If necessary, open **WorldWarIPres-YourName**.
2. Apply a transition of your choosing to all slides.
3. Make Slide 2 the active slide, display the slide master and add an animation effect of your choosing to the title placeholder and the content placeholder. For each animation, change the *Start* option to *After Previous*. Close Master view when finished.
4. Apply an animation effect of your choosing to the following objects with the *Start* option changed to *After Previous* for each object:
    Photo on Slide 2
    Explosion shape and text box on Slide 5
    Photo and text box on Slide 6
    WordArt on Slide 8
5. Set the time for all slides to remain on the screen during a slide show to *0:15* (15 seconds).
6. Change the times for three slides as follows: Slide 1 to *0:05*; Slide 5 to *0:08*; Slide 8 to *0:05*.
7. Change the *Show type* to *Browsed by an individual (window)* and turn on the *Loop continuously until 'Esc'* option in the Set Up Show dialog box.
8. Preview the slide show.
9. Save the revised presentation using the same name (**WorldWarIPres -YourName**) and then close the presentation.
10. Submit the assessment to your instructor in the manner requested.

Assessment 11.4 Creating a Self-Running Multimedia Presentation

Type: Individual or Pairs
Deliverable: Presentation with Money-Saving Strategies for College Students

1. Create a presentation with six to eight slides with your best money-saving tips for college students to help students survive on limited income while in school. Incorporate graphics, sound, and video into the presentation to make the presentation interesting and communicate your ideas.
2. Apply transition and animation effects of your choosing, setting up the slide show as a self-running presentation with appropriate times assigned for each slide.
3. Save the presentation in the Ch11 folder within the Assessments folder as **MoneyTips-YourName** and then close the presentation.
4. Submit the assessment to your instructor in the manner requested.

Assessment 11.5 Visual—Creating a Self-Running Multimedia Presentation

Type: Individual
Deliverable: Presentation about Yellowstone National Park

1. Create a presentation similar to the one shown below and on the next page in the Assessment 11.5 Yellowstone National Park Presentation with the following design specifications:
   a. The theme is Wood Type.
   b. Picture and video files to create the slides are as follows:
      Slide 2   **YellowstoneMap.gif**
      Slide 3   **OldFaithfulGeyser_nps.jpg**
      Slide 4   **GreatFountainGeyser.jpg**
      Slide 5   **InsideYellowstoneVideo.wmv**
   c. Use your best judgment to determine other formatting and alignment.
2. Apply transition and animation effects of your choosing, setting up the slide show as a self-running presentation. You determine appropriate times for each slide.
3. Save the presentation in the Ch11 folder within the Assessments folder as **YellowstoneNP-YourName**.
4. Submit the assessment to your instructor in the manner requested.
5. Close the presentation.

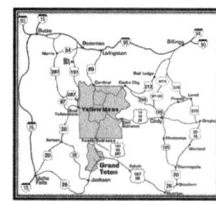

Assessment 11.5 Yellowstone National Park Presentation

continued...

Review & Assessment Chapter 11 **RA-59**

Assessment 11.5 *(continued)* **Yellowstone National Park Presentation**

Assessment 11.6 Internet Research and Composing a New Multimedia Presentation

Type: Individual or Pairs
Deliverable: Presentation about World War II

You have been asked to help the history society celebrate the 75th anniversary of World War II by creating a six- to eight-slide, self-running presentation about the war. These presentations will be loaded on kiosks placed around the school campus. Create your presentation modeled after the World War I presentation in Assessment 11.1 to Assessment 11.3. Find images, sound, and a short video clip to enhance the slides. Remember to credit the source of all multimedia. The program assistant has left you the following instructions.

1. Listen to the audio file **WorldWarII_Instructions.m4a**.
2. Complete the research, locate multimedia elements, and compose the self-running presentation. Make sure the transitions, animations, and timings are suitable for viewing by a variety of learners on the campus.
3. Save the presentation in the Ch11 folder within the Assessments folder as **WorldWarII-YourName**.
4. Submit the assessment to your instructor in the manner requested.
5. Close the presentation.

Assessment 11.7 Go Mobile—Creating a New Presentation

Type: Individual
Deliverable: Presentation about Smartphone Addiction Research

1. Open the PowerPoint mobile app and start a new blank presentation. Choose a template that you like.
2. Create slides for a presentation with research about smartphone addiction. Use the bullet points below. The first two facts are from the book *Too Much of a Good Thing: Are You Addicted to Your Smartphone?* by James A. Roberts, PhD. The last two facts are from the website https://www.bankmycell.com, an electronics recycling facilitator. You determine how to present the information. Weave into the presentation personal behaviors and observations about your own smartphone use as you complete this assessment. For example, take note as you are completing this assessment how you respond if you are interrupted by text messages or other notifications.
   - 79 percent of 18- to 44-year-olds reach for their smartphone within 15 minutes of waking every day.

- 77 percent of adults felt anxious when separated from their smartphones for a few moments.
- 85 percent of smartphone users check their device while speaking with others.
- 47 is the number of times the average smartphone user checks their device daily.

3. Add graphics, animation, and transition effects of your choosing to the presentation.
4. Use Save As to change the presentation name to **SmartphoneAddiction-YourName**, saving it in your OneDrive personal storage account.
5. Submit the presentation to your instructor in the manner requested.
6. Exit the PowerPoint mobile app.

Assessment 11.8 Job Ready—Internet Research and Composing a New Multimedia Presentation

Type: Individual, Pairs, or Teams
Deliverable: Presentation about Smartphone Policy in the Workplace

Smartphones and other wearable or mobile devices are ubiquitous, creating a unique set of issues for employers that may or may not be addressed with a smartphone policy for employees. Knowing the behaviors and safety issues related to smartphone use in the workplace that employers are concerned about will help prepare you for your next job.

1. Research information about employer management of personal smartphone use at work. Look for a sample smartphone policy and read at least two articles that discuss the issues and how employers are responding to the issues.
2. Create a presentation with an appropriate title slide followed by six slides minimum to eight slides maximum that summarize your research in bulleted lists.
3. Add a slide at the end with the URLs that you used to complete this assessment.
4. Save the presentation as **SmartphonePolicy-YourName** in the Ch11 folder in Assessments on your storage medium.
5. Submit the assessment to your instructor in the manner requested.
6. Close the presentation.

Assessment 11.9 Sending Assessment Work to OneNote Notebook

Type: Individual
Deliverable: New Page in Shared OneNote Notebook

1. Start OneNote and open the MyAssessments notebook created in Chapter 4, Assessment 4.4.
2. Make PowerPoint the active section and add a new page titled *Chapter 11 Assessments*.
3. Switch to PowerPoint. For each assessment that you completed, open the presentation, use the Export option on the File tab to create a PDF of the presentation (using the default options), and then close the presentation. Switch to OneNote. On the Chapter 11 Assessments page in the PowerPoint section in the MyAssessments notebook, insert each PDF printout in order completed.
4. Close OneNote.
5. Close PowerPoint.
6. Submit the assessment to your instructor in the manner requested.

Using and Querying an Access Database

Chapter 12

Review and Assessment

The following assessments offer opportunities to apply what you have learned in relevant, real-world situations. Save your solution files and URLs, and submit them for evaluation as directed by your instructor.

Assessment 12.1 Adding, Editing, and Deleting Records

Type: Individual
Deliverable: Locker Rentals Database (Continued in All Assessments)

1. Open **LockerRentals** and click the Enable Content button in the security warning message bar.
2. Use the *Save Database As* option in the Save As backstage area to save a copy of the database named **LockerRentals-YourName** in a new folder named *Ch12* within the Assessments folder on your storage medium.
3. Enable content in the copy of the database.
4. Open the Students table. Add a new record using StudentID *999999999*. Type your first and last names in the appropriate fields and leave all the other fields blank. Close the table.
5. Open the Rentals table and add the following new record. Close the table when finished.
RentalNumber	Tab past this field, as the number is assigned automatically by Access
LockerNumber	Select *A104* in the drop-down list
StudentID	Select *999999999 Your Name* in the drop-down list
DateRented	15sep2021
RentalPaid	Select *Yes*
DatePaid	15sep2021
6. Open the Lockers table and make the following changes to the data:
    a. Change all occurrences of *City Center* to *Downtown Campus*.
    b. Change the level number from *3* to *2* for locker numbers B108, B109, and B110.
    c. Change the locker type from *Box Size* to *Half Size* for locker numbers A101 and A102.
7. Delete the records for locker numbers A106 and C106.
8. Close the Lockers table.

- Glossary
- Infographic
- Crossword Puzzle
- Multiple Choice
- Completion
- Matching
- Assessments
- Exercises
- Projects
- Skills Exam
- Chapter Exam

9. Open the Rentals form and then add the following new record:
   - RentalNumber — Tab past this field, as the number is assigned automatically by Access
   - LockerNumber — Select *A102* in the drop-down list
   - StudentID — Select *101334799 Su-Lin Cheng* in the drop-down list
   - DateRented — 15sep2021
   - RentalPaid — Select *Yes*
   - DatePaid — 15sep2021
10. Use the Find feature to locate the record in the Locker Rentals form for locker number B100 and then delete the record.
11. Use the Find feature to locate the record in the Locker Rentals form for locker number B106 and then edit the record to show the rental was paid on *September 16, 2021*.
12. Close the Rentals form.
13. Leave the database open if you are continuing to Assessment 12.2; otherwise, close the database and submit the assessment to your instructor in the manner requested.

Assessment 12.2 Sorting and Filtering Data

Type: Individual
Deliverable: Locker Rentals Database and PDF of Filtered Table

1. If necessary, open **LockerRentals-YourName** and enable content.
2. Open the Rentals table and then sort the table by *LockerNumber* in ascending order.
3. Close the Rentals table, saving the changes to the table design.
4. Open the Lockers table and then filter the table to show only the Downtown Campus lockers.
5. With the filtered Lockers table active, create a PDF of the table by completing the following steps:
   a. Click the External Data tab.
   b. Click the PDF or XPS button in the Export group.
   c. In the Publish as PDF or XPS dialog box, navigate to the Ch12 folder within Assessments, select the current entry in the *File name* text box, and type FilteredLockersTable-YourName.
   d. Click the *Save as type* option box arrow and then click *PDF (.pdf)*. Skip this step if *PDF* is already selected as the *Save as type* option.
   e. Click the Publish button.
   f. Close the PDF window that opens to return to Access. Skip this step if the PDF document does not open in a PDF window.
   g. Click the Close button in the Close the Export – PDF dialog box that asks if you want to save the export steps.
6. Close the Lockers table. Click No when prompted to save changes to the table design.
7. Leave the database open if you are continuing to Assessment 12.3; otherwise, close the database and submit the assessment to your instructor in the manner requested.

Assessment 12.3 Creating and Editing Queries

Type: Individual
Deliverable: Locker Rentals Database

1. If necessary, open **LockerRentals-YourName** and enable content.
2. Create a query using the Simple Query Wizard using the following information. If a Microsoft Access Security Notice dialog box appears after you start the wizard with a warning that the file might contain unsafe content, click the Open button.
   a. Choose the tables and fields in this order:
      Table: Lockers   Add all fields
      Table: LockerTypesAndFees   RentalFee
   b. Choose a detail query.
   c. Change the title to *LockerListWithFees*.
3. Switch to Design view for the LockerListWithFees query and then sort the query by the *LockerNumber* field in ascending order.
4. Run the query.
5. Save and close the query.
6. Open the LockerListWithFees query and then switch to Design view.
7. Enter criteria to select the lockers in the Allen Park campus building. Run the query. Use *Save Object As* to save the revised query as *AllenParkLockers* and then close the query.
8. Open the LockerListWithFees query and then switch to Design view.
9. Enter criteria to select the lockers in the first level only of the Borden Avenue campus building. Run the query. Use *Save Object As* to save the revised query as *BordenAveL1Lockers* and then close the query.
10. Open the LockerRentals2021 query, switch to Design view, and then delete the *DateRented* column.
11. Insert a new column to the left of the *RentalPaid* column and then type the following formula in the *Field* box: Rental Fee with Tax: [RentalFee]*1.05
12. Format the *Rental Fee with Tax* column to *Currency*.
13. Run the query. Adjust the column width of the calculated column to Best Fit.
14. Save and then close the query.
15. Open the LockerRentals2021 query. Switch to Design view. Enter criteria to select only those records where the rental fee has been paid. Run the query. Use *Save Object As* to save the revised query as *PaidLockerRentals2021* and then close the query.
16. Leave the database open if you are continuing to Assessment 12.4; otherwise, close the database and submit the assessment to your instructor in the manner requested.

Assessment 12.4 Previewing and Creating PDFs of Database Objects

Type: Individual
Deliverable: PDFs of Tables and Queries in Locker Rentals Database

1. If necessary, open **LockerRentals-YourName** and enable content.
2. Open the Lockers table and then display the table in the Print Preview window.
3. Click the PDF or XPS button in the Data group on the Print Preview tab. In the Publish as PDF or XPS dialog box, navigate to the Ch12 folder within Assessments and publish a PDF of the table, naming it **LockersTable-YourName**. Close the PDF window if necessary in order to return to Access. Close the Export – PDF dialog box.

4. Close the Print Preview window and then close the Lockers table.
5. Complete steps similar to Steps 2 to 4 to create a PDF for each of the following objects, changing the file names as noted.
   Note: Consider clearing the Open file after publishing *check box in the Publish as PDF or XPS dialog box, if the box is checked, to avoid previewing each printout in the PDF window.*

Object Name	Name for PDF
Rentals table	RentalsTable-YourName
AllenParkLockers	AllenParkLockers-YourName
BordenAveL1Lockers	BordenAveL1Lockers-YourName
LockerListWithFees	LockerListWithFees-YourName

6. Create a PDF for each of the following queries by completing steps similar to Steps 2 to 4, changing the page layout to landscape orientation and the margins to *Normal*.

Object Name	Name for PDF
LockerRentals2021	LockerRentals2021-YourName
PaidLockerRentals2021	PaidLockerRentals2021-YourName

7. Leave the database open if you are continuing to Assessment 12.5; otherwise, close the database and submit the assessment to your instructor in the manner requested.

Visual Assessment 12.5 Visual—Modifying a Query to Add Criteria and a Calculation

Type: Individual
Deliverable: PDF of Query with Calculated Field

1. If necessary, open **LockerRentals-Your Name** and enable content.
2. Open the LockerListWithFees query and modify the query to create the query results datasheet shown below in the Assessment 12.5 Query with Criteria and Calculated Column datasheet. You determine the required calculated column *Field* expression as well as the criteria used to generate the query results datasheet. ***Hint:*** *The rental fee is for eight months.* Best fit the calculated column width.
3. Use *Save Object As* to save the revised query as *AllenParkAndBordenAveLockers*.

LockerNumber	LockerType	CampusBuilding	Level	RentalFee	Rental Fee Per Month
A101	Half size	Allen Park	1	$70.00	$8.75
A102	Half size	Allen Park	1	$70.00	$8.75
A103	Full Size Regular	Allen Park	1	$80.00	$10.00
A104	Full Size Regular	Allen Park	1	$80.00	$10.00
A105	Half size	Allen Park	1	$70.00	$8.75
A107	Full Size Regular	Allen Park	2	$80.00	$10.00
A108	Full Size Regular	Allen Park	2	$80.00	$10.00
A109	Full Size Wide	Allen Park	2	$95.00	$11.88
A110	Full Size Wide	Allen Park	2	$95.00	$11.88
A115	Full Size Regular	Allen Park	2	$80.00	$10.00
A120	Full Size Regular	Allen Park	2	$80.00	$10.00
B100	Full Size Regular	Borden Avenue	1	$80.00	$10.00
B101	Box Size	Borden Avenue	1	$65.00	$8.13
B102	Box Size	Borden Avenue	1	$65.00	$8.13
B103	Full Size Regular	Borden Avenue	1	$80.00	$10.00
B104	Full Size Wide	Borden Avenue	1	$95.00	$11.88
B105	Full Size Wide	Borden Avenue	1	$95.00	$11.88
B106	Full Size Regular	Borden Avenue	1	$80.00	$10.00
B107	Box Size	Borden Avenue	1	$65.00	$8.13
B108	Full Size Wide	Borden Avenue	2	$95.00	$11.88
B109	Full Size Wide	Borden Avenue	2	$95.00	$11.88
B110	Box Size	Borden Avenue	2	$65.00	$8.13

Assessment 12.5 Query with Criteria and Calculated Column

4. Create a PDF of the query, naming it **AllenParkAndBordenAveLockers-YourName** and saving it in the Ch12 folder within the Assessments folder. Make sure the datasheet fits on one page.
5. Close the query and then close the LockerRentals database.
6. Submit the assessment to your instructor in the manner requested.

Assessment 12.6 Job Ready—Researching Data for a New Database

Type: Individual, Pairs, or Teams
Deliverable: Data for a New Database (Continued in Chapter 13, Assessment 13.6)

In preparation for your job search after graduation, you decide to research organizations in your field of study and assemble the data you will need to facilitate contacting each organization for employment. *Note: In this assessment, you are preparing data only. You will create a new database to store the data after you complete the topics in Chapter 13.*

1. Research organizations in your field of study that would be suitable to contact for employment. Record each organization name, mailing address, email address, telephone number, and department you would contact. Include any other information about the organization that would be helpful to you for employment opportunities. Your goal is to assemble data for a minimum of 10 organizations.
2. Create a worksheet in Excel that resembles an Access datasheet to store the data. Start the data in cell A1 and do not leave any rows or columns blank within the data. The first-row column headings will become field names when you create the database in the next chapter. Make sure to type the data immediately below the column headings. The worksheet will be imported into Access in Assessment 13.6.
3. Rename the Sheet1 tab to *Contacts*.
4. Save the Excel workbook as **JobSearchContacts-YourName** in the Ch12 folder in Assessments on your storage medium.
5. Submit the assessment to your instructor in the manner requested.

Assessment 12.7 OneNote—Sending Assessment Work to OneNote Notebook

Type: Individual
Deliverable: New Page in Shared OneNote Notebook

1. Start OneNote and open the MyAssessments notebook created in Chapter 4, Assessment 4.4, if the notebook is not currently open.
2. Make Access the active section and type Chapter 12 Assessments as the page title.
3. For each PDF you created in an assessment in this chapter, insert the PDF on the Chapter 12 Assessments page. If you completed all assessments, insert the PDFs in this order:
   FilteredLockersTable-YourName
   LockersTable-YourName
   RentalsTable-YourName
   AllenParkLockers-YourName
   BordenAveL1Lockers-YourName
   LockerListWithFees-YourName
   LockerRentals2021-YourName
   PaidLockerRentals2021-YourName
   AllenParkAndBordenAveLockers-YourName
4. Close OneNote.
5. Submit the assessment to your instructor in the manner requested.

Creating a Table, Form, and Report in Access

Chapter 13 Review and Assessment

The following assessments offer opportunities to apply what you have learned in relevant, real-world situations. Save your solution files and URLs, and submit them for evaluation as directed by your instructor.

Assessment 13.1 Creating a New Database File and Creating Tables

Type: Individual
Deliverable: Home Listing Database (Continued in Assessment 13.2)

1. Create a new blank database file **Listings-YourName** in a new folder named *Ch13* in the Assessments folder on your storage medium.
2. Add these fields in the blank Table1 datasheet (keep the default *ID* field, too):

Field Name	Data Type	Caption
SoldDate	Date & Time	Date Sold
SalePrice	Currency	Sale Price
Commission	Number	Commission Rate
SellingAgent	Short Text	Selling Agent

3. Adjust column widths so that all column headings are entirely visible.
4. Save the table as *Sales* and then close the table.
5. Create a new table in Design view using these field names and data types:

Field Name	Data Type
ListingID	Short Text
AgentID	Short Text
StreetAdd	Short Text
ClientLName	Short Text
ClientFName	Short Text
ListDate	Date/Time
AskPrice	Currency
HomeType	Short Text

6. Assign *ListingID* as the primary key field.
7. Save the table, naming it *Listings*, and then close the table.
8. Create a third table in the database using the following field names. All the fields are the Short Text data type. You decide the view in which to create the table.
   Field Name
   AgentID (assign this field as the primary key)
   LName
   FName
9. Save the table as *Agents* and then close the table.

- Glossary
- Infographic
- Crossword Puzzle
- Multiple Choice
- Completion
- Matching
- Assessments
- Exercises
- Projects
- Skills Exam
- Chapter Exam

10. Leave the database open if you are continuing to Assessment 13.2; otherwise, close the database and submit the assessment to your instructor in the manner requested.

Assessment 13.2 Adding Fields, Modifying Field Properties, and Creating a Lookup List

Type: Individual
Deliverable: Home Listing Database and PDFs of Tables (Continued from Assessment 13.1)

1. If necessary, open **Listings-YourName** and enable content.
2. Open the Listings table, make *ClientFName* the active field, and add a new Short Text field named *ContactPhone*.
3. Switch to Design view and then create a lookup list for the *HomeType* field with the following list entries. Make *Single family home* the default value for the field.
   Single family home
   Condominium
   Townhouse
   Duplex
   Triplex
   Fourplex
   Other
4. Save the table and then switch to Datasheet view. Adjust the column widths as needed so that all column headings and the default value for the *HomeType* field are entirely visible, and then close the table, saving changes to the layout.
5. Open the Sales table and then add a new Yes/No field named *SplitComm* to the end of the table. Add a caption to the field with the text *Split Commission?* and then adjust the column width to show the entire column heading.
6. Switch to Design view, make *Commission* the active field, and then change the following field properties:
   a. Type .05 in the *Default Value* property box.
   b. Change the Field Size property option to *Double*.
   c. Change the Decimal Places property option to *2*.
   d. Change the Format property option to *Percent*.
7. Change the field name of the *ID* field to *ListingID* and then change the data type from *AutoNumber* to *Short Text*.
8. Save and close the Sales table.
9. Open the Agents table. Add the following captions to the fields and adjust column widths in Datasheet view so that all column headings are entirely visible. Close the table when finished, saving changes to the layout.

Field Name	Caption
AgentID	Agent ID
LName	Agent Last Name
FName	Agent First Name

10. Open the Agents table and add a new record in the table with your name and with *10* as the *Agent ID*.
11. Open the Listings table and add the following record:

ListingID	2021-1	ContactPhone	800-555-3225
AgentID	10	ListDate	03/15/2021
StreetAdd	98 First Street	AskPrice	87500
ClientLName	Jones	HomeType	Condominium
ClientFName	Marion		

12. Open the Sales table and add the following record:
ListingID	2021-1	*Commission Rate*	5.00%
Date Sold	03/22/2021	*SellingAgent*	10
Sale Price	82775	*Split Commission?*	Yes

13. Display each table datasheet in Print Preview and then create a PDF of the datasheet using the following file names and saving in the Ch13 folder in Assessments:

Table Name	Name for PDF
Agents	Agents-Your Name
Listings (landscape; normal margins)	Listings-Your Name
Sales (normal margins)	Sales-Your Name

14. Close the **Listings-YourName** database.
15. Submit the assessment to your instructor in the manner requested.

Assessment 13.3 Editing Relationships, Creating a Form and a Report

Type: Individual
Deliverable: Home Listing Database and PDFs of New Objects (Continued in Assessments 13.4 and 13.5)

1. Open **HomeListings**.
2. Use Save As to *Save Database As*, naming the copy **HomeListings-YourName** in the Ch13 folder within the Assessments folder on your storage medium.
3. Enable content in the copy of the database.
4. Display the relationships.
5. Edit each relationship to turn on *Enforce Referential Integrity*. With the Relationships window still open, capture an image of your screen and paste the image into a new Word document. Save the Word document as **Relationships-YourName** and save it in the Ch13 folder in Assessments. Use the Export option on the File tab to create a PDF of the document, using the same file name. Close the PDF window if the window opens, close Word, and then close the Relationships window.
6. Create a form using the Form tool for the Listings table and then modify the form as follows:
    a. Change to a theme of your choosing.
    b. Insert the image **ForSale.jpg**. Change the Size Mode property to *Zoom*, the Width to 1.5 inches, and the Height to 1 inch.
    c. Change the font size for the title text to a size of your choosing.
    d. Make any other changes you think improve the appearance of the form.
    e. Save the form using the default form name and then close the form.
7. Reopen the form and then display the first page in Print Preview. Change the margins to *Normal*. Click the Page Setup button in the Page Layout group on the Print Preview tab and then click the Columns tab in the Page Setup dialog box. Change the *Width* in the *Column Size* section to 7.5 inches and then click OK. Create a PDF of the *first page only* of the form, naming the PDF **ListingsForm-YourName** and saving it in the Ch13 folder in Assessments. *Hint: Use the Options button in the Publish as PDF or XPS dialog box to choose the* Page(s) *From:* 1 *to* 1 *option before clicking the Publish button*. Close the form.
8. Create a report using the Report tool for the Sales table and then modify the report as follows:
    a. Insert the **ForSale.jpg** image, applying the same changes as those applied to the picture in the form.
    b. Change the title text to a font size of your choosing.
    c. Resize controls as needed so that all objects fit on one page.

d. Make any other changes you think will improve the appearance of the report.
   e. Save the report using the default report name.
9. Create a PDF of the report, naming it **SalesReport-YourName** and saving it in the Ch13 folder in Assessments. Close the report.
10. Leave the database open if you are continuing to Assessment 13.4; otherwise, close the database and submit the assessment to your instructor in the manner requested.

Assessment 13.4 Compacting on Close and Backing Up a Database

Type: Individual
Deliverable: Home Listing Database (Continued from Assessment 13.3, and Continues in Assessment 13.5)

1. If necessary, open **HomeListings-YourName** and enable content.
2. Turn on the *Compact on Close* option for the database.
3. Create a backup copy of the database, accepting the default file name and saving in the default folder.
4. Leave the database open if you are continuing to Assessment 13.5; otherwise, close the database and submit the assessment to your instructor in the manner requested.

Assessment 13.5 Visual—Creating a Query and Report

Type: Individual
Deliverable: PDF of Report (Continued from Assessment 13.4)

1. If necessary, open **HomeListings-YourName** and enable content.
2. Create a query using all the fields in the Sales table. Insert a calculated column titled *Amount* between *Commission Rate* and *Selling Agent* as shown in the Assessment 13.5 Sales Commissions Report below. You determine the field expression and format. Save the query, naming it *SalesCommissions*. Close the query.
3. Create a report similar to the Assessment 13.5 Sales Commissions Report shown below, based on the SalesCommissions query. Use your best judgment to determine the formatting options by examining the Assessment 13.5 Sales Commissions Report and by exploring the four Report Layout Tools tabs. Save the report using the default name.
4. Display the report in Print Preview and open the Page Setup dialog box with the Columns tab active. Change the *Width* in the *Column Size* section to 8 inches. Create a PDF of the report in portrait orientation and with narrow

Sales Commissions

ListingID	Date Sold	Sale Price	Commission Rate	Amount	Selling Agent	Split Commission?
2018-1	3/22/2018	$82,775.00	5.00%	$4,138.75	Student last name	☑
2018-3	3/31/2018	$59,000.00	4.00%	$2,360.00	Davidson	☑
2018-4	3/30/2018	$72,000.00	5.00%	$3,600.00	Polaski	☑
2018-7	3/31/2018	$74,500.00	5.00%	$3,725.00	Ungar	☑
2018-9	3/25/2018	$64,500.00	5.00%	$3,225.00	Antoine	☑

Assessment 13.5 Sales Commissions Report

margins, saving it as **SalesCommissions-YourName** in the Ch13 folder within Assessments.
5. Close the report and then close the database.
6. Submit the assessment to your instructor in the manner requested.

Assessment 13.6 Job Ready—Creating a New Database

Type: Individual, Pairs, or Teams
Deliverable: New Database for Job Search (Continued from Chapter 12, Assessment 12.6)

In preparation for your job search after graduation, you assembled data from at least 10 organizations in your field of study. You will create a new database for storing and maintaining the data.

1. Create a new blank database file **JobSearchContacts-YourName** in the Ch13 folder in Assessments on your storage medium.
2. Import the worksheet created in Assessment 12.6 into the Access database to create a new table by completing the following steps:
   a. Close the Table1 datasheet created by Access in the new database.
   b. Click the External Data tab, click the New Data Source button in the Import & Link group, point to *From File*, and then click *Excel*.
   c. In the first Get External Data - Excel Spreadsheet dialog box, click the Browse button, navigate to the Ch12 folder in Assessments and then double-click *JobSearchContacts-YourName.xlsx*.
   d. Click OK and then click the Open button if the Microsoft Access Security Notice dialog box appears.
   e. Click Finish in the Import Spreadsheet Wizard dialog box to accept all default options for importing the Excel worksheet into a new table. If any error messages occur, the most likely cause is that the Excel worksheet has blank rows or columns within the data. Start Excel, open the Excel workbook and then make corrections to ensure the data begins in cell A1 and no blank rows or columns exist within the data. Save the revised workbook, return to Access, and then try again to import the worksheet.
   f. Click the Close button in the Get External Data - Excel Spreadsheet dialog box.
3. Open the Contacts table in Design view and review each field and its field properties. Make the email address field the primary key.
4. Create a report from the table using the Report tool. Make any changes you think are necessary to improve the appearance of the report. Adjust column widths as necessary to ensure all data is visible and that the report looks professional in Print Preview.
5. Create a PDF of the report, saving it as **Contacts-YourName** in the Ch13 folder within Assessments.
6. Close the report and then close the database.
7. Submit the assessment to your instructor in the manner requested.

Assessment 13.7 Sending Assessment Work to OneNote Notebook

Type: Individual
Deliverable: New Page in Shared OneNote Notebook

1. Start OneNote and open the MyAssessments notebook created in Chapter 4, Assessment 4.4, if the notebook is not currently open.
2. Make Access the active section and add a new page titled *Chapter 13 Assessments*.
3. For each PDF you created in an assessment in this chapter, insert the PDF on the Chapter 13 Assessments page.

If you completed all assessments, insert the PDFs on the OneNote page in this order:
Agents-YourName
Listings-YourName
Sales-YourName
Relationships-YourName
ListingsForm-YourName
SalesReport-YourName
SalesCommissions-YourName
Contacts-YourName
4. Close OneNote.
5. Submit the assessment to your instructor in the manner requested.

Integrating Word, Excel, PowerPoint, and Access Content

Chapter 14 Review and Assessment

The following assessments offer opportunities to apply what you have learned in relevant, real-world situations. Save your solution files and URLs, and submit them for evaluation as directed by your instructor.

Assessment 14.1 Importing and Exporting Data with Access and Excel

Type: Individual
Deliverable: Database and Worksheet with Used Books List

1. Start Access and then open the **UsedBooks** database.
2. Use Save As to save a copy of the database as **UsedBooks-YourName** in a new folder named *Ch14* within Assessments.
3. Enable Content in the copy of the database.
4. Import the Excel workbook **BookList** in the Ch14 folder in StudentDataFiles using the option *Append a copy of the records to the table* [Books] in the Get External Data – Excel Spreadsheet dialog box. Do not save the import steps.
   Note: Only two dialog boxes are required in the Import Spreadsheet Wizard when you use the Append *option.*
5. Open the Books table when the import is complete, review the datasheet, and then close the table.
6. Create a query in Design view, adding the Books table and the Students table to the query and with the following fields in order:

Field Name	Table Name
BookID	Books
FName	Students
LName	Students
Title	Books
Author	Books
Condition	Books
AskPrice	Books
StopPrice	Books

7. Save the query as **BookList** and then run the query.
8. Review the query results datasheet and then close the query.
9. Export the BookList query to Excel, saving the workbook as **ExportedBookList-YourName** in the Ch14 folder within Assessments. Select the options to export data with formatting and layout information and to open the destination when the export is complete.
10. Make the following changes to the worksheet in Excel:
    a. Change each occurrence of *Jane Doe* to your first and last names in the *First Name* and *Last Name* columns.

- Glossary
- Infographic
- Crossword Puzzle
- Multiple Choice
- Completion
- Matching
- Assessments
- Exercise
- Project
- Skills Exam
- Chapter Exam

b. Change the orientation to *Landscape*.
   c. Make sure all columns will fit on one page.
   d. Create a header with the sheet tab name at the upper center of the page and a footer with your name at the bottom center of the page.
11. Save the revised workbook using the same name (**ExportedBookList-YourName**) and then close Excel.
12. Close the Export - Excel Spreadsheet dialog box without saving the export steps, close the database, and then close Access.
13. Submit the assessment to your instructor in the manner requested.

Assessment 14.2 Embedding Data with Word and Excel

Type: Individual
Deliverable: Document with Embedded Tables from Excel

1. Start Word and then open **StatCounterTables**.
2. Use Save As to change the file name to **StatCounterTables-YourName**, saving in the Ch14 folder within Assessments.
3. Start Excel and then open **SocialMediaStats**.
4. Select and copy A4:B9.
5. Switch to Word and position the insertion point at the left margin two line spaces below the first paragraph. Use *Paste Special* from the Paste button arrow to open the Paste Special dialog box. Select *Microsoft Excel Worksheet Object* in the *As* list box and then click OK to embed the worksheet data.
6. Center the embedded worksheet object.
7. Embed C4:D9 from the Excel worksheet into the Word document, inserting the object a double-space below the last paragraph in the document.
8. Center the embedded worksheet object.
9. Edit both embedded objects to display two decimal places after each percent value. **Hint:** *Before ending editing of each embedded object, make sure the cells displayed in the editing window are only the cells that were copied.*
10. Add your name to the bottom of the document a double-space below the embedded cells.
11. Save the revised document using the same name (**StatCounterTables-YourName**) and then close Word.
12. Close Excel. Click Don't Save if prompted to save changes to the worksheet.
13. Submit the assessment to your instructor in the manner requested.

Assessment 14.3 Linking Data between Word and Excel

Type: Individual
Deliverable: Document with Linked Excel Charts

1. Start Word and then open **StatCounterCharts**.
2. Use Save As to change the file name to **LinkedStatCounterCharts-YourName**, saving in the Ch14 folder within Assessments.
3. Start Excel and then open **SocialMediaStats**.
4. Use Save As to change the file name to **LinkedSocialMediaStats-YourName**, saving in the Ch14 folder within Assessments.
5. Select, copy, and link the *Global Market Share* pie chart to the Word document a double-space below the first paragraph. Select the option to link using the destination theme. Center the chart in the document.
6. Select, copy, and link the *United States Market Share* pie chart to the Word document two line spaces below the last paragraph. Select the option to link using the destination theme. Center the chart in the document.

7. Turn on the option for each linked object to automatically update.
8. Add your name in a footer in the document.
9. Save the revised document using the same name (**LinkedStatCounterCharts-YourName**) and then close the document. Leave Word open.
10. Make the following changes to the data in the Excel worksheet:

Cell Address	Current Entry	New Entry
B5	65.3	60.4
D5	60.5	45.8
B8	8.5	13.4
D7	5.8	8.5
D8	8.0	20.0

11. Save the revised workbook using the same name (**LinkedSocialMediaStats-YourName**) and then close Excel.
12. With Word active, open **LinkedStatCounterCharts-YourName** and choose Yes when prompted to update links. Save and then close the document after updating links and exit Word.
13. Submit the assessment to your instructor in the manner requested.

Assessment 14.4 Visual—Embedding Excel Data in PowerPoint

Type: Individual
Deliverable: PowerPoint Presentation with Embedded Excel Data

1. Start PowerPoint and then open **TopVacDestinations**.
2. Modify the presentation to resemble the one shown in the Assessment 14.4 Vacation Destinations Survey Results presentation on the next page, using the following information:
   a. The tables on Slide 2 and Slide 3 are embedded from the Excel worksheet **VacDestinations**.
   b. Edit the embedded objects to appear as shown in the Assessment 14.4 presentation. Use your best judgment to match colors and borders.
   c. Add Slide 4 as a new slide.
   d. Add the image shown on the title slide by searching in Online Pictures using the keyword *luggage*, or by inserting the student data file **luggage**.
3. Save the revised presentation as **TopVacDestinations-YourName**.
4. Close PowerPoint and Excel.
5. Submit the assessment to your instructor in the manner requested.

Assessment 14.5 Creating a Video from a Presentation

Type: Individual
Deliverable: Video from a Presentation

1. Start PowerPoint and then open **PaintedBuntingForExport**.
2. Create a video from the presentation using the *HD (720p)* option and with the recorded timings in effect. Save the video in the Ch14 folder in Assessments as **PaintingBuntingVideo-YourName**.
3. Close PowerPoint when the video is complete. Click the Don't Save button if prompted to save changes to the presentation.
4. Submit the assessment to your instructor in the manner requested.

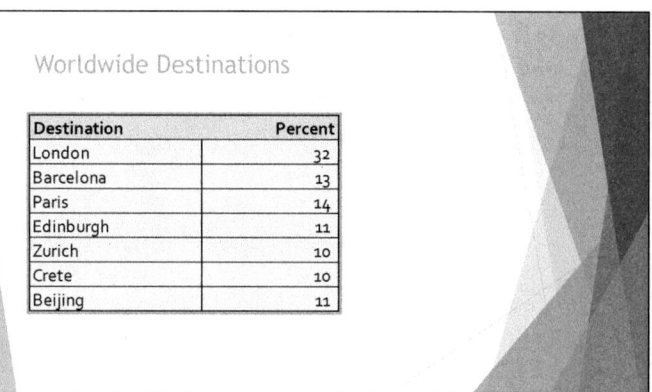

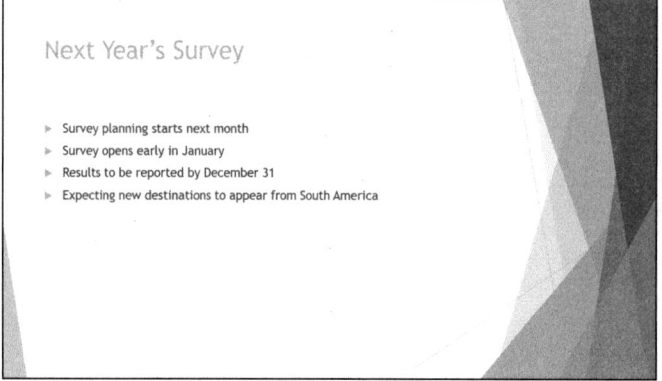

Assessment 14.4 Vacation Destinations Survey Results Presentation

Assessment 14.6 Job Ready—Researching 5G, Creating a Word Outline, and Importing Outline into Presentation

Type: Individual, Pairs, or Teams
Deliverable: Presentation on the Benefits of 5G

Assume that you are preparing for a job interview for a position as a technology blogger. You want to impress the hiring committee with your research and writing skills about technology topics.

1. Research the benefits of 5G cellular networks and how 5G connectivity is expected to benefit society as carriers upgrade their networks to the new standard.
2. Create a Word document in an outline format with the text you want to include in a presentation. Apply heading styles as needed for exporting a Word outline to PowerPoint.
3. Save the Word document as **Outline5GPres-YourName** and then close Word.
4. Start PowerPoint and create a new presentation. Add a title slide with an appropriate title and subtitle. Import the Word document saved in Step 3 to new slides. Enhance the presentation as needed.
5. Save the presentation as **5GOverview-YourName** in the Ch14 folder within Assessments.
6. Close the presentation and close PowerPoint.
7. Submit the assessment to your instructor in the manner requested.

Assessment 14.7 Sending Assessment Work to OneNote Notebook

Type: Individual
Deliverable: New Page in Shared OneNote Notebook

1. Start OneNote and then open the MyAssessments notebook created in Chapter 4, Assessment 4.4, if the notebook is not currently open.
2. Make Integrating the active section and then type Chapter 14 Assessments as the page title.
3. Open the following files in the source application and use the *Export* option to create a PDF. Ensure each document and worksheet is scaled to fit one page. In OneNote, on the Chapter 14 Assessments page in the Integrating section in the MyAssessments notebook insert each PDF printout in order completed.
   ExportedBookList-YourName from Excel.
   StatCounterTables-YourName from Word.
   LinkedStatCounterCharts-YourName from Word.
   TopVacDestinations-YourName from PowerPoint, with publish options set to format the slides as handouts with four slides horizontal per page.
   PaintedBuntingVideo-YourName inserted as a linked file.
   5GOverview-YourName from PowerPoint, with publish options set to handouts with six slides horizontal per page.
4. Close OneNote and any other open applications.
5. Submit the assessment to your instructor in the manner requested.

Using Office Online and OneDrive

Chapter 15
Review and Assessment

The following assessments offer opportunities to apply what you have learned in relevant, real-world situations. Save your solution files and URLs, and submit them for evaluation as directed by your instructor.

- Glossary
- Infographic
- Crossword Puzzle
- Multiple Choice
- Completion
- Matching
- Assessments
- Chapter Exam

Assessment 15.1 Creating a Document with Word Online

Type: Individual
Deliverable: Document in OneDrive

1. Open a browser window and sign in to OneDrive.
2. Start a new blank document in Word Online and then type the following text using the default settings.
   What Is Office 365?
   Office 365 is the subscription-based model for purchasing Office. An Office 365 Home subscription offers up to six users Office applications from the cloud for all their devices. One user can be signed in on up to five devices at the same time. At OneDrive, registered users have access to web-based editions for Word, Excel, PowerPoint, Outlook, and OneNote. According to Microsoft, these are the additional benefits included with an Office 365 subscription:
   - desktop applications for Publisher and Access
   - 1 TB storage for each person
   - 60 Skype world minutes per month for each person
   Because Office 365 is hosted by Microsoft as a cloud computing technology, the software will always be up to date and accessible from any device with an internet connection. Office 365 is ideal for consumers with multiple devices who want to view or edit documents from any location at any time.
   Purchasing an Office 365 subscription is an option that home users may want to consider. Keep in mind that to continue using the software, the subscription fee must be paid monthly or annually. Whether the cost will be less expensive over the long run depends on the number of traditional software licenses you would buy and whether you upgrade immediately to new releases. Finally, consider whether you need the additional options that the subscription is offering. For example, if you do not use Access, Publisher, or Skype, the additional benefits are not meaningful to you.
3. Perform a spelling check and carefully proofread the document.
4. Apply formatting options of your choosing to improve the appearance of the document.
5. Search for and insert a suitable picture at the bottom center of the document.
6. Rename the document **Office365-YourName** and then close the document tab.
7. Submit the assessment to your instructor in the manner requested.

Assessment 15.2 Creating a Worksheet in Excel Online

Type: Individual
Deliverable: Workbook in OneDrive

1. With OneDrive open, start a new blank workbook in Excel Online and then set up the following information in a worksheet. You determine the worksheet layout.

Cost Comparison for Office 365 and Office Desktop Edition Subscription fee versus standard software license for each PC			
Office 365 Home		Office Desktop PC	
Monthly subscription fee	11	Office Home and Student license fee	199.00
Estimated years to subscribe	4	Number of licenses to buy	3
TOTAL COST FOR OFFICE 365		TOTAL COST FOR OFFICE DESKTOP	
Difference in cost Office 365 versus Office Desktop licensing			

2. Create formulas to calculate the total cost of Office 365, the total cost of Office Desktop, and the difference between the two pricing models.
3. Apply formatting options of your choosing to improve the appearance of the worksheet.
4. Rename the workbook **Office365CostComparison-YourName** and then close the workbook tab.
5. Submit the assessment to your instructor in the manner requested.

Assessment 15.3 Creating a Presentation in PowerPoint Online

Type: Individual
Deliverable: Presentation in OneDrive

1. With OneDrive open, start a new blank presentation in PowerPoint Online.
2. Select a theme and variant of your choosing.
3. On Slide 1, type What Is Office 365 Home? as the slide title and your name as the subtitle.
4. Add a minimum of two slides to the presentation, with text that you compose that summarizes the main points from the text that you typed in Assessment 15.1. For example, on Slide 2, explain the cloud-based subscription model of purchasing Office 365; and on Slide 3, provide a list of what is included in an Office 365 Home subscription.
5. Apply formatting options of your choosing to enhance the presentation.
6. Rename the presentation **Office365Pres-YourName** and then close the presentation tab.
7. Submit the assessment to your instructor in the manner requested.

Assessment 15.4 Downloading Assessment Files and Managing Files

Type: Individual
Deliverable: Downloaded Assessment Files on a Storage Medium; Word Document with Screen Images of File Lists in OneDrive

1. With OneDrive open, select and download **Office365-YourName**.
2. Select and download **Office365CostComparison-YourName**.
3. Select and download **Office365Pres-YourName**.

4. Use File Explorer to create a new folder named *Ch15* within Assessments on your storage medium and then copy and paste the three files downloaded from OneDrive in Steps 1 through 3 into the new folder. Close the File Explorer window when finished.
5. In OneDrive and with *Files > Documents* displayed in the Content pane, click <u>New</u> in the bar along the top of the window and then click <u>Folder</u>. Type <u>C15-Assessments</u> as the folder name and click <u>Create</u>.
6. Select and move the files created from Assessments 15.1, 15.2, and 15.3 to the C15-Assessments folder.
7. With *Files > Documents* the active list displayed in OneDrive, create another new folder, *C15-Topics*.
8. Select and move the three files created from the topics in this chapter to the C15-Topics folder.
9. Capture an image of your desktop with *Files > Documents* active in your OneDrive account. Start a new Word document using the desktop edition (not Word Online) and paste the image.
10. Switch back to OneDrive, click the C15-Assessments folder tile, and then capture an image of your desktop with the folder contents displayed. Paste the image into the Word document below the capture pasted in Step 9. Refer to Assessment 1.1, Step 6 (Workbook, Chapter 1), if you need assistance capturing a screen image.
11. Switch back to OneDrive and display *Files > Documents* in the content pane, then click the C15-Topics folder tile. Capture an image of your desktop with the folder contents displayed and then paste the image into the Word document below the capture pasted in Step 10.
12. Save the Word document as **OneDriveFiles-YourName** in the Ch15 folder within Assessments on your storage medium and then close Word.
13. Submit the assessment to your instructor in the manner requested.

Assessment 15.5 Visual—Creating a Document

Type: Individual
Deliverable: Document in OneDrive

1. Start a new Word Online blank document to create the text and image shown in the Assessment 15.5 document on the next page.
2. Rename the document **CloudComputing-YourName**.
3. The font used is 12-point Book Antiqua with double spacing. Search for the image using the phrase *cloud computing*, or insert the image using the student data file **cloud-computing.png**.
4. When the document is complete, download a copy of the document to the Downloads folder.
5. Open a File Explorer window and copy **CloudComputing-YourName** from the Downloads folder to the Ch15 folder within Assessments on your storage medium.
6. Sign out of OneDrive.
7. Submit the assessment to your instructor in the manner requested.

Assessment 15.5 *CloudComputing-YourName* **Document in Word Online**

Jobs ▸ Assessment 15.6 Job Ready—Researching The Differences in Office Editions

Type: Individual, Pairs, or Teams
Deliverable: Document or Presentation on Key Differences in Office Editions

You are preparing for a presentation to the office manager who has expressed concern that she does not understand the differences between Office software purchased as a one-time desktop license and the subscription-based Office 365.

1. Research the various ways to buy Office and the differences in how the software installs on each device for a desktop version and a subscription version. Include in your research a comparison of the features offered in each edition and whether a continuous internet connection is required to use the applications with the Office 365 edition.
2. Create a document or presentation that summarizes the results of your research.
3. Save the document or presentation as **OfficeEditions-YourName** in the Ch15 folder within Assessments.
4. Submit the assessment to your instructor in the manner requested.

Assessment 15.7 Sending Assessment Work to OneNote Notebook

Type: Individual
Deliverable: New Page in Shared OneNote Notebook

1. Start OneNote and open the MyAssessments notebook created in Chapter 4, Assessment 4.4 if the notebook is not currently open.
2. Make OneDrive the active section and then type Chapter 15 Assessments as the page title.

3. Open the following files in the desktop version of the source application and use the Export option to create a PDF. Ensure each document and worksheet is scaled to fit one page. In OneNote, on the Chapter 15 Assessments page in the OneDrive section in the MyAssessments notebook, insert each PDF printout in order completed.
    Office365-YourName from Word.
    Office365CostComparison-YourName from Excel.
    Office365Pres-YourName from PowerPoint, with publish options set to format the slides as handouts with four slides horizontal per page.
    OneDriveFiles-YourName from Word.
    CloudComputing-YourName from Word.
    OfficeEditions-YourName from Word or PowerPoint (with publish options as handouts with four slides horizontal per page).
4. Close OneNote and any other open applications.
5. Submit the assessment to your instructor in the manner requested.